BTEC Introduction

IT @ Work

Veronica White

www.heinemann.co.uk
✓ Free online support
✓ Useful weblinks
✓ 24 hour online ordering

01865 888058

Inspiring generations

Heinemann Educational Publishers
Halley Court, Jordan Hill, Oxford OX2 8EJ
Part of Harcourt Education

Heinemann is the registered trademark of
Harcourt Education Limited

Text © Veronica White, 2004

First published 2004

09 08 07 06 05 04
10 9 8 7 6 5 4 3 2 1

British Library Cataloguing in Publication Data is available
from the British Library on request.

ISBN 0 435 46246 6

Designed by Kamae Design
Typeset by Wearset Ltd, Boldon, Tyne and Wear

Original illustrations © Harcourt Education Limited, 2004

All photographs by Gareth Boden

Cover design by Wooden Ark Studio

Cover photo: © Getty Images

Printed in the UK by Bath Press Ltd

Acknowledgements
Every effort has been made to contact copyright holders of material reproduced in this book. Any
omissions will be rectified in subsequent printings if notice is given to the publishers.

Contents

Introduction

This book takes you through the units of the Edexcel Level 1 BTEC Introductory Awards in IT @Work. It also includes guidance on skills that you will need to complete many of the units, and the scheme as a whole. These include organising your work area and files; saving; printing; making screen prints; and guidance on making presentations. Each unit includes the coverage of the skills required, as well as exercises to provide evidence of having carried out the work.

The software used in this book is Microsoft Windows XP and Microsoft Office Professional XP. If you are not using the same software then your screens will look different.

   ## The Scheme

There are two levels in the qualification: the certificate is a 180-hour course, and the diploma is a 360-hour course. The certificate is nested within the diploma and can be taken as a one or two year course.

The scheme offers an introduction to IT and the opportunity to develop personal skills and confidence in your ability to work, learn and achieve your potential at level 1. The aim is to encourage and acknowledge achievement in those who may:
- be aged 14 to 19 and want to follow a vocational course; have gained some qualifications at entry level; or have limited achievement at GCSE grades D to G.
- wish to make a fresh start that offers a different learning and assessment style.
- be over 19 and intend to return to education and training or prepare for employment.

Aims

The scheme is designed to:
- develop the skills, techniques, personal qualities and attitudes needed for success at work and to help your employment prospects
- develop your ability through study, and offer a stepping stone into employment in IT
- provide a suitable qualification to move on to a range of further study at levels 1 and 2.

Design and structure

The qualifications are made up of vocational core units, personal skills units and vocational option units. The core units provide an introduction to the IT sector and the basic skills required to work in it. The personal skills units are to help you to prepare for work.

To achieve the **Certificate**, you must complete **four** units. Each unit has either 30 or 60 guided learning hours. Core Unit 3 is a 60-hour unit, as are all the vocational units.

Unit   Title

Core: the core units are compulsory:
   1   Starting Work in the IT Industry
   3   Developing Skills in IT

Personal skills: choose **one** of these units:
   4   Personal Effectiveness
   5   Social Responsibility at Work
   6   Financial Management

Vocational options: choose **one** of these units:
   7   PC Systems
   8   Using the Internet
   9   IT Applications
   10   Digital Devices

To achieve the **Diploma**, you must complete eight **units**. Each unit has either 30 or 60 guided learning hours. Core Unit 3 is a 60-hour unit, as are all the vocational units.

Unit   Title

Core: the core units are compulsory:
   1   Starting Work in the IT Industry
   2   Working in IT
   3   Developing Skills in IT

Personal skills: choose **two** of these units:
   4   Personal Effectiveness
   5   Social Responsibility at Work
   6   Financial Management

Vocational options: choose **three** of these units:
   7   PC Systems
   8   Using the Internet
   9   IT Applications
   10   Digital Devices

Assessment and grading

All units except the personal skills units are graded as pass, merit or distinction. Personal skills units are only graded as pass.

For the Certificate, Unit 1 is externally assessed. For the Diploma, Units 1 and 2 are externally assessed. The external assessment will be a project for which the centre can select the setting. Each candidate *might* have a different setting. The work will be internally assessed and a BTEC external assessor will check the assessment and grading. The remainder of the units are assessed internally.

You must achieve a pass grade in each unit to qualify for a qualification grade. Your certificate will show a qualification grade of pass, merit or distinction. For the Certificate, this will be decided by the better performance of the two 60-hour units. For example, if you get a merit in Unit 3 and a distinction in Unit 7, you will get a qualification grade of distinction. For the Diploma, the qualification grade will be drawn from the best performance from two of the four 60-hour units. For example, if you get a pass in Unit 3 and a distinction in Unit 7, you will get a qualification grade of merit.

The personal skills units and the externally assessed units do not contribute to the qualification grade.

Adult literacy, adult numeracy and key skills

The scheme includes mapping of adult literacy, adult numeracy and key skills at level 1. The adult skills are for post-16 candidates only. The key skills are:

- application of number
- communication
- information technology
- improving own learning and performance
- problem solving
- working with others.

These are different qualifications. If certification is required candidates must be registered separately.

Using your computer

This section gives you information that you will need for many of the units.

Organising files on your computer

It is necessary to create a structured and organised filing system on your computer so that you know where your work is. It is also important to download files in a way that keeps them organised and protects you from viruses. **Use this rule:** if you have to scroll to see the contents of a folder, create new (sub)folders.

The easiest way to organise your files is by their purpose. Windows automatically creates a My Documents folder that programs such as Word and Excel try to save your files into, so this is a good place to begin. Create (sub)folders within the My Documents folder which identify their contents, such as: Finance, College, Companies, etc. Each should have an obvious purpose. You can subdivide the folders further if you need to.

If you download a lot of information from the Internet – and you may while carrying out some of the units in this qualification – decide where you will keep this information and create the folders so that you know where to save them.

Saving

Before you save decide on two things: the filename and the location.
- Give the file a name you can remember – something you will recognise later.
- Decide where you are going to store the file, thinking about both the drive and the folder.

1) Select **Save As** from the **File** menu. The Save As dialogue box is displayed (see Figure i).
2) Select the location and make sure it is displayed in the **Save in** box.
3) Enter the filename in the **File name** box.
4) Select the file type from the drop-down menu in the **Save as type** box.
5) Click the **Save** button.

When you start to save you may see a message displayed saying that the filename already exists. If so, give the file a different name.

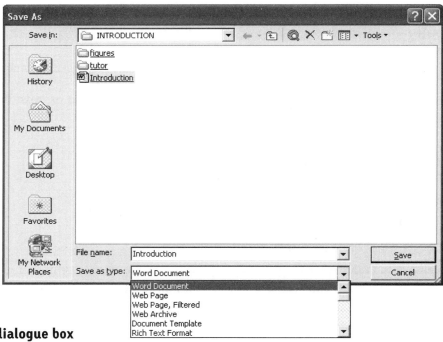

Figure i The Save As dialogue box

Printing

Remember that ink and paper are expensive so before you print you should check your work on screen for accuracy. You should also use the spellcheck and preview facilities on the toolbar to check your work (see Figure ii).

Previewing will show you how many pages your document contains and how it will look. Print only the pages you need.

If the work only just carries over to a second page, use the Shrink to Fit button in the Preview screen toolbar to automatically fit it all on one page.

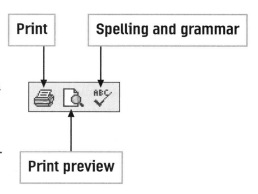

Figure ii Toolbar options for checking work before printing

Making screen prints

In some units, you are asked to make screen prints to show evidence that you have carried out tasks, and to illustrate points in the user guides you are asked to produce. To do so:

1) Make sure the evidence or screen you require is displayed.
2) Press the key marked **PrtScr** or **PrintScrn** on your keyboard.
3) Open Word, and a blank document should appear on your screen.
4) Click on the right mouse button, click **Paste**.
5) A "picture" of the screen you selected will be displayed (see Figure iii).
6) If it is to be used as evidence of activities carried out, add your name and the date.
7) If it is to be used as part of a user guide, you can crop the picture – highlight the image by clicking on it.
8) Select the crop tool from the picture toolbar (see Figure iv).
9) Remove the sections of the image that you do not require.

Figure iii Making a screen print

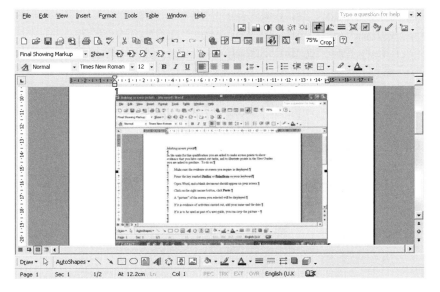

Figure iv Selecting the crop tool

# Preparing presentations

Today, many job interviews require candidates to give a presentation. Public speaking is a skill that is increasingly required in business. However, it can be intimidating. Tools such as Microsoft PowerPoint can add a lot of interest to a presentation, but you should explore the program and use it fully.

Content

Think about how you are going to use a presentation program. Most people just use bullet points – and they use too many. You should keep bullet points simple, perhaps five words per line, and five points per slide.

You should include facilities such as graphs (to illustrate figures and comparative data), images (to identify products or components), and other facilities such as organisation charts, as appropriate.

Audience notes can be useful as they allow members of the audience to add their own notes and comments as you go through your presentation. If you use audience notes, make sure you include pauses so that the audience can add their own notes. Hand-outs containing further information are also useful. Use these materials carefully: audience notes and handouts should never distract the audience from your presentation because they are too busy reading or writing. You should probably give additional notes at the end of your presentation.

You also need to think about your audience. Do they know anything about the subject already? Is it appropriate to use humour?

Delivery

Your delivery skills are just as important as the content of your presentation. It is essential that you appear confident and energetic.

- Speak slowly and clearly. Avoid "um" and "you know" as they create an impression of uncertainty. Practice the presentation out loud to get used to your own voice.
- Stand up straight and smile – it makes you appear more confident. Standing up gives the best impact, and helps your breathing, which will be affected by your nerves.
- Do not fiddle with your hair, your glasses, your notes or the coins in your pocket. This is distracting to the audience.
- Make eye contact – the audience needs to feel that you are paying attention to them before they will pay attention to you.

unit 1

Starting work in the IT industry

This unit has been designed to help you to see what it is like to work in the IT industry. You will think about your skills and qualities, and how you will go about getting the kind of job you think you would like to do. The focus is on what you could do when you have finished this qualification, and what you can do next.

You will look at jobs that are available, investigate the skills needed to carry them out, and the training required to do them. You will investigate the skills required to build and run IT systems including:

- technical support
- network support
- hardware engineering
- software and website design
- selling
- marketing.

In this unit you need to learn about:

- the different types of jobs available within the sector
- the different types of organisation and venues in the sector
- the relationship between lifestyle and job choices.

 Different types of jobs

If you want to work in the IT industry it is important to think about the type of job that you want to do and the skill level and experience you will need in order to achieve that position. You may want to work in a technical support or network support role, or you may prefer selling or marketing. You may want to work for an international company, or you may want to work for yourself offering your services to other companies.

Whatever decisions you make, you will also have to consider the effect a particular job will have on your lifestyle. For example, the effect that travelling to different locations around the country, or even around the world may have on your home life.

Whatever position you may want to achieve, it is important to think about the type of job in which you will start, and what you need to do, including further training and on the job experience, in order to achieve that goal.

Types of jobs

There are a number of different types of jobs.

• • • *Part-time work*

This is a job where you work for a limited number of hours per week or month. If full-time members of staff work 35 hours per week, a part-time member of staff may work, say, 20 hours per week.

• • • *Full-time work*

This is a job where you work for a specified number of hours per week or month, often around 35 hours per week, but often more.

• • • *Temporary work*

This is a job where you work for a limited period of time for a company. It may be for 6 months or a year, but the time period is specified when you start the work. Although the job is temporary it may be full-time or part-time.

• • • *Seasonal work*

This is a job where you work for a limited period of time for a company, similar to a temporary position. This type of job is related to industries that show seasonal variations, such as tourism, or perhaps a job related to a season such as Christmas.

• • • *Permanent work*

This is a job where you work for a specified number of hours per week or month, on a long-term basis – i.e. the time period is not set when you begin the job. Although the job is permanent it may be full-time or part-time.

• • • *Casual work*

This is a job where you work for a limited number of hours per week or month on a 'when required' basis. You may be called upon by the company when they need your services.

• • • *Skilled work*

This is a job where you require specific skills to carry out the work. For example, if you wanted to work as a network manager you would require knowledge of network systems.

• • • *Unskilled work*

This is a job where you do not require any specific skills to carry out the work.

Job titles and job roles

There are numerous jobs in IT. Each type is necessary to the others, but different skills and knowledge are needed for each.

• • • *Users*

By far the largest group consists of those who use IT to perform tasks. They use commercial software such as word processing, spreadsheets, database managers, accounting programs, and many others.

• • • *Programmers*

This group either create programs that do not yet exist, or amend existing programs. The programs can be very simple or extremely complex.

• • • *Analysts*

This group looks at the requirements of the users and designs systems to meet the needs of the process.

• • • *Engineers*

Computers are machines, and any machine can break. There is, therefore, a need for people to repair them. Upgrading computers is also a common requirement that may involve adding more memory, installing a new interface card, or installing a faster processor. This group of people needs to know about the inner workings of the computer, and about electronics.

• • • *Designers*

This group can be broken down into two:

1) A relatively small number of people who design new computers and their components. They design new and ever more powerful processors, video

display components, and whole computer systems. They require technical skills and an extensive knowledge of electronics, digital logic, semiconductor physics, and a number of related subjects.

2) People who design and develop products such as new games and websites.

Each of these groups can work in different areas, including:
- administration
- design
- marketing and selling and service industry.

IT administration

This area may include:
- managing the computer system, the resources such as components, sites, communications, and the people required for associated roles
- running the day-to-day operations to keep systems available for the users, including providing technical support to run the systems and engineering to update, upgrade and maintain them
- organising the resources required for the systems, locations and people.

Jobs in this area include:

• • • *Systems manager*

This is the person who is in charge of a system that a company depends upon to carry out its business, making long-term decisions about policy, usage and strategic planning.

• • • *Technical assistant*

This is the person who helps in the day-to-day running of a system, carrying out routine operations to ensure that the system is available to users.

• • • *Help desk assistant*

This is the person who answers queries from IT users on a variety of subjects. The user may be able to resolve some of the problems themselves. If they are not able to resolve a query, they must know who else to bring in to resolve the problem.

• • • *Network manager*

This is the person who is in charge of the network that a company depends upon to carry out its business, making long-term decisions about policy, usage and strategic planning.

• • • *Network administrator*

This is the person who helps in the day-to-day running of a network, carrying out routine operations to ensure that the network is available to users.

• • • *IT buyer*

This is the person who is in charge of the purchasing of IT equipment and systems, making long-term decisions about policy, usage and strategic planning.

• • • *Purchase assistant*

This is the person who helps in the day-to-day purchasing of equipment, systems and supplies, carrying out routine tasks to ensure that the necessary items are available for users.

• • • *Systems analyst*

This is the person who looks at the procedures and systems that are required in a business, and designs a system to ensure that the work is carried out in the correct sequence and at the correct time.

IT designers

This area may include:

- designing new computers and their components
- designing whole computer systems
- designing software for users
- designing new games and websites.

Jobs in this area include:

• • • *Web designer*

This is the person who looks at the business requirements of advertising the company and its services on the Internet and produces suitable material to meet the company requirements.

• • • *Multimedia developer*

This is the person who develops materials including text, images and audio using a variety of media.

• • • *Game designer*

This is the person who designs new games, or develops existing material in line with the advances in technology.

• • • *Programmer*

This is the person who creates the code or instructions that make up a program. The program may be to meet any need within a company from Payroll to Purchasing.

● ● ● *Desktop publisher*

This is the person who draws together (or develops) text documents, images and other objects and formats them to produce published materials.

● ● ● *E-learning content developer*

This is the person who designs and develops the content to be used in e-learning.

● ● ● *Digital technology jobs, i.e.:*

- *film processing*: the person who, using suitable machinery, processes film
- *photo finishing assistants*: the person who assists in the procedures for processing film.

IT marketing and selling and service industry

This area may include:

Marketing
- developing the company's IT marketing strategy
- product development: market research to determine the demand for products and services
- comparison studies of competitors
- identifying potential customers
- developing publicity programs for a target audience
- clarifying or justifying the company's point of view on health or environmental issues
- evaluating advertising and promotion programs
- noting social, economic, and political trends that might affect the company
- making recommendations to enhance the company's image.

Sales
- determining the company's sales strategy
- overseeing, or being part of the sales force to meet the sales plan
- preparing work schedules and assigning work.

Jobs in this area include:

● ● ● *Marketing manager*

This is the person who is in charge of the marketing plans and strategy, making long-term decisions about policy on how the company, its image, and its products will be positioned in the marketplace. Marketing managers develop pricing strategy with the intention of getting the highest market share possible.

● ● ● *Marketing assistant*

This is the person who helps in the day-to-day tasks to promote the company and its products or services in the marketplace.

• • • *Sales assistant*

This is the person who helps in the day-to-day tasks to sell the company products or services.

• • • *Call handling assistant*

This is the person who helps in the day-to-day tasks to assist customers with queries about the company products or services.

▨▨▨ EVIDENCE ACTIVITIES

Job advertisements

You are going to look at the types of job available and investigate the requirements.

1   Choose three of the jobs above that you think you might like to do. Select one from each section — Administration, Designers, and Marketing and selling and service industry.

2   Find advertisements for the type of job you selected. You can look on the Internet or in newspapers.

3   Draw up a list of the skills, qualities and qualifications required.

Planning ahead

1   Are there jobs available that you could apply for now?

2   If not, why do you not meet the requirements?

3   What can you do about it?

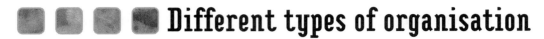 # Different types of organisation

Categories

There are a number of different types of organisation. Most organisations are permanent, but the personnel are often *contracted* to carry out specific activities for a specified period of time. Some companies, rather than use their own personnel to carry out certain activities, will *outsource* the work to a company that specialises in providing the service required – this is quite common in the IT industry.

Nature of business

Organisations are run in different ways:

● ● ● *Public sector*

This is a local or national government body that provides a service for the general public – such as the police.

● ● ● *PLC*

This is a private limited company, which is an organisation that has shareholders. They have limited liability for any debts. Profits are dispersed among them and are referred to as dividends. These companies operate in a number of different fields.

● ● ● *Charity*

This is an organisation where any funds are used to help the 'cause'. For example, the NSPCC uses the funds and donations it receives to help children.

● ● ● *Partnership*

This is an organisation where more than one person (and up to 20) work together. They share the profit, but are also responsible for each other's debts. They are often groups in professions such as solicitors.

● ● ● *IT consultancy*

This is an organisation where one or more consultants provide IT services to another company, institution or person. Consultants (or contractors) are often self-employed.

● ● ● *Retail*

This is an organisation that sells goods to the public.

Scale of organisation

Organisations can be:

● ● ● *Local*

These are organisations based in one town or city only. They are usually small-scale companies (with one or more outlet), schools, colleges and clubs.

● ● ● *Regional*

These are organisations based in one region or county. They include companies such as the regional or county council and small county-based or regional organisations.

● ● ● *National*

These are organisations based in many different locations all around the country. They have a corporate image and identity that is immediately identifiable. They include companies such as Boots, Dixons, Tesco and Barclays Bank.

● ● ● *International*

These are organisations based in many different countries around the world. They have a corporate image and identity that is immediately identifiable. They include companies such as IBM, Microsoft, Cisco and Oracle. One of the most easily identifiable is probably MacDonalds.

▢▢▢ EVIDENCE ACTIVITY

Identifying organisations

1   Name three organisations in each of the following types: local; regional; national; international.

2   What kind of organisations are they? How are they run? What size? What location?

3   Describe three different organisations that operate in the IT sector.

4   Describe an organisation where you could find a job you would like to do.

 Lifestyle

This is about your way of life, your standard of living, the level of comfort you want. Many people think it is related to your wealth, income and resources. It is often thought about in terms of material goods and possessions, but it is also about what you want – your aspirations (ambitions, goals and objectives), and your health, wellbeing and happiness. The way you live now may influence the choices you make when choosing a job.

• • • *Striking a balance*

Many people want to improve their standard of living but feel that they are on a treadmill that goes faster and faster. Life today seems to be blurring the lines between work life and home life. Many people are successful in work, but forget their health. So much is required that they eat on the run, and do not take time to exercise, or de-stress. If you have a busy schedule you must learn to manage stress and look after yourself. Lifestyle is about balancing the demands of work and home and getting them into perspective.

You have to decide on your own measure of success – what makes you happy. Some people want to move away from a frenetic lifestyle and focus instead on personal values. A growing number want a slower and simpler life. People are realizing that they do not feel fulfilled with more and bigger and better. Although you have to earn enough money, you also have to live within your means to be able to work less and have time for what you value. It is important to choose your lifestyle rather than going through life on automatic pilot dictated by a job.

• • • *Making choices*

You should think about what you are, and are not, prepared to do to earn your living. These choices will help to determine your job and lifestyle. For example, while some people are happy to work night shifts because they earn more money, others choose not to. The list below gives some of the reasons why people earn more money.

- There is a high level of skill required for the job.
- You need certain qualifications to do the job.
- The job requires a long period of training. During this training you may earn a relatively small amount, but the rewards are greater when the training is completed.
- You may be required to work unsociable hours.
- You have a high level of seniority and responsibility within the company.
- You have a long service period with the company.
- There are regional differences in income.
- You have opportunities to earn overtime or bonuses.
- The demand for the type of labour is high and a scarcity of people who can do it.

GIVE IT A GO · lifestyle choices

Think about the list on page 10. Would you be prepared to earn more money with a company for the each of the reasons given? For example, would you stay with a company for a long period of time? Explain why you would – or would not.

▣▣▢ EVIDENCE ACTIVITIES

Lifestyle and work

1   Describe the lifestyle you would like, by making up two lists under the headings **Things you need** and **Things you want**.

2   How would these things affect your job choice?

Choosing a job to fit a lifestyle

Your class should split up into groups of four or five. Each group should discuss these questions and make notes on the findings of the group:

1   What different lifestyle priorities could a person have regarding each of these items?
   - *Flexibility of location*: Are they prepared to travel? How far? How often? Would they be prepared to move to another location?
   - *Social aspirations*: What are their ambitions, goals and objectives? How will they achieve them?
   - *Personal relationships*: Consider the personal relationships now and in the future that you hope to develop. How will your lifestyle affect these relationships?
   - *Social reasons for working*: Make a list of the reasons for working (other than earning money) such as meeting other people.

2   How will each of these lifestyle choices affect the kind of job the person will want?

3   Each group should report its findings to the remainder of the class. Students should keep a neat copy of their group findings in their evidence folder.

Organisations and lifestyle

1   Briefly describe three different types of organisation.

2   Explain why working in each of these organisations might affect your lifestyle.

Jobs

We all need to earn a living, but choice of job can affect lifestyle. Before you decide on the type of job you would like, you need to consider not only your personal skills and qualities and whether they match the requirements of the position, but also your personal and professional ambitions – will this job satisfy these ambitions?

GIVE IT A GO investigate jobs

You will find this section easier to understand if you talk to any people you know who work in IT, and ask them how they progressed to their position. You may be able to visit an organisation in your area which provides IT services, or ask any such organisations to send a speaker to talk to you about the industry. Many large organisations can provide such speakers.

• • • *Hours of work*

The hours you are required to work vary depending on whether the job is full-time or part-time. If you are working part-time you will probably be working about 20 hours per week. If you are working full-time you will work around 35 hours per week (about seven hours per day, five days a week). Starting and finishing times vary depending on the type of business, whether the company allows flexitime working (see Unit 2 page 17) or whether there is a shift-working pattern. Shift working allows varying patterns – sometimes three shifts (06.00 to 14.00, 14.00 to 22.00, 22.00 to 06.00) or three 12-hour days, followed by three 12-hour nights, followed by three days off.

• • • *Personal skills and qualities*

Professional qualifications

In deciding what job you want to do, it is important to find out whether you need professional qualifications in order to be considered for it. One way of finding out is to look at job advertisements for the kind of job you are interested in and identifying any qualifications that are specified for the position. You can then find out how you go about getting those qualifications.

Career planning

If you want to work in the IT field you should do some career planning. This includes choosing the kind of job you want to do. Your next step will be to get that first job, and then develop towards your goal. You may change jobs before you reach your goal. You need to consider the steps you need to take:

- Gather information about your interests, values, skills – that you have now, and that need to be developed.
- Explore the occupations you are interested in, and research the jobs in which you would like to work. Finally, research the employment market. You should get more specific information after you narrow down your options by job shadowing, part-time work, and volunteering.
- Identify and evaluate possible occupations and explore alternatives. Choose both a short-term and a long-term option.

- Carry out further investigation in order to reach your goal. This would include: investigating sources of additional training and education; developing a job search plan; preparing your CV and covering letters; job searching; gathering information on companies and doing some preparation for interviews.

These topics are covered in other units including Unit 4 – which will help you to explore your potential. You can find more details about gathering the information on your vocational, personal, interpersonal, and transferable skills as well as your interests.

Self-assessment

Unit 4 includes guidelines and exercises to help you with self-assessment. You are given guidance on values and interests, your personality traits and skills – including how to identify your strengths and weaknesses and then match them to positions that may be available in the IT sector. You should look at Unit 4 for guidance on gathering information about yourself.

Personal qualities

Before deciding on a job, you should consider your personal qualities, preferences and skills. For example:

- Do you like dealing with the public (in which case a job in sales, as a helpdesk or call centre assistant, or as a systems analyst might suit) or do you prefer working alone (in which case working as a programmer may be more suitable)?
- Do you have physical and other limitations that might make the job more difficult? For example, poor eyesight might make using a screen all day more difficult.
- Are you calm and reflective or are you a more volatile personality? Can you deal with stressful situations (such as constant complaints if you are working on a helpdesk) and not allow your own stress levels to be affected?

■■■ EVIDENCE ACTIVITY

Personal skills, qualities and qualifications

Outline the type of job you would like and explain why (personal skills and qualities) and how (qualifications and experience) you can get that job.

If you are not sure, this might be a good starting point:

Imagine you have just woken up.

▷ You have to dress for work. What will you wear — formal or casual clothes?

▷ How do you get to work — public transport, car, or walk?

▷ What does your place of employment look like — is it a modern open–plan office building?

▷ Once in work, what are you going to do — do you have your own office? Are you giving the orders? Are you working in a team?

unit 2

Working in IT

In this unit you will learn about working in IT, and about being at work in general. You will look at what the terms and conditions of employment are — knowing the rules about employment should help when you are looking for a job. You will also learn about induction — the period when you start work, and how you will be monitored in your work.

In this unit you will need to learn about:

- the terms and conditions of different types of job
- the induction and training process
- procedures used to monitor performance.

Terms and conditions

Employment

The agreement between you and your employer – the Terms of Employment – gives details of the tasks and responsibilities you are expected to carry out and what you will receive for doing so, in terms of wages, benefits and bonuses. Details are often outlined in a:

• • • *Job description*

This is a general outline that will include: your job title; the details of your duties and responsibilities; the place and department in which you will work; the supervision and assessment arrangement for that job.

• • • *Job specification*

This is a more detailed statement based on the job description, and includes qualities required such as: responsibilities; qualifications and experience; skills needed and characteristics considered important.

• • • *Contract of employment*

This is a document that the employer is required to give you, detailing your terms of employment. It includes: your job title; hours of work; holiday arrangements; rate of pay; when and how you are paid; period of notice by the employer and employee; grievance details; legal rights. The length of employment will be included if you are on a short-term contract. It should include annual leave (holiday) entitlement.

Your contract of employment comes into existence as soon as you start work, and in doing so, you indicate that you accept the job on the terms offered by the employer.

• • • *Staff handbook*

This outlines the company procedures and rules. It gives information about the company and your role. It gives the rules and your responsibilities. For example, what your responsibilities are regarding computer security.

• • • *Short-term employment contracts and flexibility*

Today there are far more jobs offered on short-term employment contracts. This allows more flexibility for the employer. They can employ people with the skills they require during a project for a fixed period, and they do not then have to find other work for them when that phase of the project has been completed.

In recent years employers expect far more flexibility from the workforce. The hours you work may be related to the job you are doing – for example, if you work in a support role you may have to start early and finish late on different days and maybe have to work at the weekend or on public holidays.

GIVE IT A GO ## Contract of Employment

If you could write the Contract of Employment for your own job what would it include?

Pay

You can be paid for the work that you do in a number of ways. You will know from your contract what you are paid per hour and how many hours you are expected to work. You may be paid for the hours you have worked weekly or monthly. At one time if you were paid weekly it was referred to as *wages*, and if you were paid monthly it was *salary*.

Whatever the frequency of your pay, you may be paid in cash, by cheque or directly into an account such as your bank or building society. Weekly pay is more likely to be in cash, whereas it is unusual for monthly payments not to be paid directly into an account. You may be paid by cheque for expenses you have incurred on behalf of the company such as travel and accommodation.

• • • *National Minimum Wage Act 1998*

This ensures that certain age groups earn at least a specified minimum amount per hour. All businesses must pay at least the minimum wage. The rates for the past few years are shown below, but note that the rates for 1 October 2004 are, as yet, provisional.

	UNDER 18	**18–21**	**22 AND OLDER**	**22+ TRAINING**
1 Oct 2002	N/A	£3.60	£4.20	£3.60
1 Oct 2003	N/A	£3.80	£4.50	£3.80
1 Oct 2004	possibly	£4.10	£4.85	£4.10

Work patterns

The majority of people work what is referred to as *regular* hours – 9 to 5. Many positions in IT have, and continue to require, irregular work patterns. These jobs are usually linked to engineering and maintenance work (such as doing system backups) or may be support roles (such as fault resolution). This may include working shifts or simply covering early starts and late finishes.

Many companies have adopted a more flexible approach to employment:

● ● ● *Flexitime employment*

Here you are required to work the same number of hours in the week or month, but you have some flexibility as to when you are in the workplace. There are usually *core* hours – hours when you must be in work. For example, a company may decide that the core hours are 09.30 to 16:30, with permissible time between 07:30 and 18:30. This would mean that on any day you can work the number of hours required at any time between 07:30 and 18:30, but you must be no later starting than 09:30 and you cannot finish before 16:30. You may also be able to build up the hours you have worked so that you can take an extra day off each month.

● ● ● *Shift patterns in employment*

It may be that an employee works, say, three days on, two days off, and then three nights. This type of work schedule is less likely now in IT. At one time it was quite common for operators (the people who worked in large mainframe rooms) to work this type of pattern. Now most of this work has been automated. There are few companies running their systems on mainframe computers.

● ● ● *Self-employment*

Many people in the IT industry are self-employed. They would normally work on short-term contracts within a company, and then move on to another company when that work is completed.

Holidays

You have a statutory entitlement to 4 weeks' paid holiday each year. This must be taken during the holiday year, and there is no right to carry over holidays. You must be notified in writing of the start date of the holiday year. Many employers give bank holidays and other public holidays in addition to the normal holiday entitlement, but there is no legal requirement for them to do so.

Changes to laws relating to special leave for the family came into effect on 6 April 2003. There were changes to the rules for maternity leave as well as the introduction of rights to paid adoption and paternity leave, and rights for parents of young children.

● ● ● *Maternity leave*

This includes the right to time off for antenatal care and two weeks' compulsory leave after the birth. There are conditions that have to be met to receive pay, but women are entitled to 26 weeks' **ordinary** maternity leave, regardless of how long they have worked for their employer. Ordinary maternity leave is normally paid leave. **Additional** maternity leave starts immediately afterwards and continues for another 26 weeks. It is usually unpaid.

• • • *Paternity leave*

This is a type of paid leave that must be started within eight weeks of the birth or adoption, and taken as either a one- or two-week period.

• • • *Adoption leave*

This is available to individuals who adopt, or one partner of a couple if the couple adopt jointly. The other member of the couple has the right to paternity leave and pay.

• • • *Parental leave*

Both mothers and fathers who have completed one year's service are entitled to 13 weeks' (unpaid) parental leave to care for their child. It can usually be taken up to five years from the birth – or in adoption, five years from the placement date.

Parents of disabled children are entitled to 18 weeks' leave up to the child's 18th birthday.

All employees are allowed to take a reasonable amount of unpaid time off work to deal with family emergencies. Such time may be used to deal with an unexpected or sudden problem such as a dependant becoming ill or having an accident, or the death of a dependant.

• • • *Flexible working*

Parents of children aged under six, or of disabled children aged under 18, have the right to apply to work flexibly. The employer has a duty to consider such requests seriously.

The parent only has the right to *request* flexible working hours, but the employer has to fully justify the reason if refusing it.

• • • *Other leave*

If you are required to attend court for jury service or as a witness, you will usually be given leave. Your company does not have to pay you, but you will be paid allowances by the court.

You can use your paid annual leave to carry out your duties if you are in the reserved armed forces. Any further time off is at the discretion of your employer, and will be unpaid leave.

Practices

• • • *Pension rights*

There are four types of pension:

Personal pension
A personal pension plan is an investment policy designed to give a lump sum and income in retirement. They are available to any UK resident under 75-years-old. They can be bought from insurance companies, banks, investment organisations and even some retailers – such as supermarkets and high street shops.

You pay money into a plan, the money is invested and a fund is built up. The amount of money available when you retire depends on: the amount of money paid in; how well the funds perform; and the annuity rate on the retirement date – which means the factor used to convert the money into a pension.

Occupational pension

These are set up by employers to provide income for their employees when they retire. The employer sets up the scheme, but it is run by a board of trustees that is responsible for ensuring payment. Some occupational pensions are salary-related. This means that the amount you get depends on the number of years you have been a member of the scheme, and on your final earnings. Others are run on a money-purchase basis, in which the contributions are invested and used to buy a pension when you retire. The amount you get from this type of pension scheme depends on the amount of money paid in and how well it has been invested.

State pension

State pension provision in the UK is in two parts: the Basic State Pension and the Second State Pension (S2P).

The Basic State Pension is a flat-rate pension payable from State pension age – currently 65 for men and 60 for women, although the retirement age for women will gradually change to 65. The amount you receive depends upon your National Insurance contributions. To get the full basic state pension you should have credits for approximately 90 per cent of your working life, otherwise you will get a smaller pension based on your credits.

S2P is a State pension in addition to the basic pension and it depends on your earnings. It was previously known as the State Earnings Related Pension Scheme (SERPS). Only people paying class 1 National Insurance contributions can contribute. Benefit is only paid from State pension age.

Stakeholder pension

A new scheme, introduced by the government on 6 April 2001. It is intended to provide a low-cost way of saving. Employers do not have to join the scheme.

The employee decides on the amount, but the minimum is £20 a month. The employer does not have to make any contribution but may choose to do so. The money is taken directly from your wages.

• • • *Health schemes*

Many companies offer free membership of private health schemes to their employees. This means that you can get private care in hospitals, dental care, and a range of other health services.

• • • *Health and safety*

Your employer has a duty to ensure that you have a safe environment in which to work, and also that you are aware of health and safety requirements within the company.

Benefits

There are a number of benefits that employers offer their employees. Although the amount of pay is not increased, help with some of the items that have to be paid for on a daily basis such as travel, food, and clothing costs are considered to be benefits. These include:

• • • *Meals on duty*

This means that the employee is provided with meals during working hours. The alternative to providing free meals is the use of a subsidised canteen. This means that the employer pays for a proportion of the running costs of the facility and the employees are offered meals at a lower cost.

• • • *Season ticket loans*

A season ticket costs less than paying for a journey each day. However, the cost of a season ticket can be high. Some employers offer their employees a loan to cover the cost of the season ticket for travel to and from work.

• • • *Use of facilities*

These may include sports and social club facilities that may be provided free of charge, or at a reduced rate compared to commercially provided facilities.

• • • *Free clothing*

This may be a uniform for jobs such as in the police or fire service. Many employers also provide specialist equipment that is required to carry out jobs, free of charge. This may include protective clothing or specialist footwear.

• • • *Bonuses*

These may be paid to employees as an incentive to, say, meet sales targets.

• • • *Skills development*

Many employers pay for training for their employees. Most training is directly related to the job, but employers also pay for courses relating to the individual – such as personal effectiveness. Some employers pay for *any* training that a employee wishes to undertake, in the belief that it adds to their wellbeing and that happy employees are more productive employees.

• • • *Working away*

Most companies offer incentives to employees who have to work away from home for periods of time. They will normally pay for all accommodation costs as well as food and travel.

●●● *Discounts*

If applicable, a company may offer reduced prices for their products or services.

●●● *Benefits and tax*

Some of these benefits are taxable – such as a company car if it is used for private use, and medical insurance.

Non-taxable benefits include:
- meals taken in a staff canteen
- car parking at or near your place of work
- nursery places in the workplace for employees' children only
- relocation expenses up to a limit of (currently) £8,000.

■■■ EVIDENCE ACTIVITY

Contract of Employment

Ask three or four people who you know (some working in the IT field) if they have a Contract of Employment. Ask them if you can look at it. If this is not possible contact a few companies (not all in the IT sector), explain what you are doing and ask them if it is possible for you to have a sample Contract of Employment.

1   Compare the examples. Outlines are enough, for example, how the jobs are paid.

2   What are the similarities?

3   Are there any differences in the terms and conditions of jobs in the IT sector? Explain what the differences mean, for example, weekly and monthly pay.

4   If there are differences, explain what they are.

■ ■ ■ ■ Induction and training

GIVE IT A GO   starting work

> You may find it useful to arrange a visit to a local business with your group, or perhaps to ask someone to come in to talk to you about how organisations work. You will get a broader picture if you ask people you know what it is like in their workplace.

When you start work you should already know something about the company – you should have done some research for your interview. When you are interviewed for a job you should ask questions such as, which department will you be working in, whether you will be working in a team or by yourself and who will you be reporting to.

• • • *Induction*

When you start a new job there is a mixture of excitement, anticipation and anxiety about what is in store for you. You may be concerned about whether you are up to the job, whether people will like you, how to work the coffee machine, and whether you will make a fool of yourself on the first day.

The first opportunity a company has to work with new employees is at induction training. During this period you will find out a lot more about the company. Because it is required by law, you should get instruction on health and safety, and fire regulations.

Many new starters find their first experiences in a company difficult – for example, getting to know routines, finding their way around, meeting new people, and knowing what is expected of them. There is a lot to take in. The more you get people involved in the process, the more successful it will be.

The company needs you to learn and understand their methods of doing things – their procedures. This helps the company to ensure that their business runs efficiently and effectively.

One of the problems with induction training is that new starters are expected to understand and retain a lot of information. The intention is to help new starters become familiar with the company, learn who they are working with, understand the company vision, and feel part of the team.

Staff handbook

The staff handbook may be issued and used during induction to help you to get to know the contents. It will contain details of the company procedures – for example, grievance, disciplinary and appraisal procedures. It will include your responsibilities – what the company expects of you. There will be information about the company holiday allowance and the procedures when you are sick or absent from work for any other reason.

You should check the details when you start work. Departments or teams usually ask that only a certain number of staff take holidays at the same time. This is to allow the department to continue to carry out its functions while members of staff take holiday. You should check in your department who, exactly, you should contact if you are unable to attend work. You should be clear about the length of time you can be away from work before you need a self-certification note or a medical note.

Dress code

Most companies want to project a professional business image. They operate some standard of dress and appearance. Dress code may be dictated by the nature of the work being carried out. You should dress in a manner that is suitable and appropriate to the business.

In some jobs you will have to wear a uniform during working hours. If so, it will usually be provided by the company. You may be required to wear smart clothing. Jeans, shorts, t-shirts and trainers may not be acceptable.

What may be a suitable dress code for one business may be entirely inappropriate for another. Various industries have specific requirements, and it is reasonable to impose rules to comply with health and safety requirements. For example, in food preparation and catering hair must be tied back and covered, and jewellery may not be worn.

Employers who have a dress code to project an image must ensure that it does not place unnecessary demands on employees. Nor should a code be based just on tastes and preferences. Where employees do not come into contact with the public the dress code may be more relaxed. Many young and creative companies do not impose any dress code.

GIVE IT A GO   legal requirements

In companies, some procedures are for the organisation itself, and some are legal requirements.

1   Which procedures are legal requirements?

2   Describe these procedures.

3   Why are they important?

Training

As part of the induction process, or at other times, your company may require you to receive training of one sort or another. There are many types of training. Your company may want to upgrade your job skills or your personal skills. There may also be some types of training that they are required to do by law, such as Health and Safety training. Here are some of the different ways your company may want to train you.

• • • *Health and Safety training*

Depending on the type of company there may be a requirement to provide specific Health and Safety training. This should be dealt with in such a way that you understand the relevance to your job. It will probably include responsibilities and procedures, what to do in a case of emergency, etc., for items such as:

• *Handling heavy equipment*: Training should be given to all employees involved in handling heavy equipment. Risk assessment should be carried out to minimise the risk of injury and to identify the hazards involved. Suitable precautions should be taken to avoid and reduce risks – these should be included in safe working procedures.

• *Dangerous substances*: Companies usually include procedures for risk assessment and safe working procedures in induction training. If your job involves dealing directly with dangerous substances then you should receive full and appropriate training. Dangerous substances are found in many workplaces. Exposure to them can happen in factories, shops, and offices, not just at obvious locations such as chemical plants. They can cause health problems from cancer to skin irritations. Harm can occur from a single short exposure or by long-term accumulation of substances in the body. A recent survey of European workers found that 16 per cent reported handling hazardous products and 22 per cent reported being exposed to toxic vapours.

• • • Technical updates

These come from the product manufacturer and give details of any changes to products – it may be the specification, or the performance.

• • • Trade conferences

These gather together all interested parties within a business sector. They provide demonstrations and exhibitions of the latest developments. Companies can exhibit their products and services. They are a good way of getting a lot of information in one place at the same time. You should try to keep up with new equipment and technologies. You can then point out the advantages that can be offered to the company, staff and customers. One way of doing this is to attend trade conferences.

• • • Vendor briefings

These allow companies to meet directly with their customers. Discussions may be about the latest products and developments. It is an opportunity to resolve problems, not only with the product, but also with things like delivery and maintenance.

▢▢▢ EVIDENCE ACTIVITIES

Induction training

1 Why do employers have induction training?

2 Why is it important for companies to carry out induction training?

3 Why is it important for you to have induction training?

Report about induction

Choose an organisation where you have personal experience or know an employee (or make polite enquiries explaining what you are doing), and ask them about induction at their company.

Write a report about induction at that organisation.

Induction process

1 Explain how your employer can use the induction process to help you to understand the terms and conditions of your employment.

2 What might be used to help in this process?

Procedures used to monitor performance

Appraisal

The purpose of appraisal should be to evaluate progress. If you are expected to perform to standards, you have to know what they are, and how well you are meeting them. To achieve this, your employer can include a job description in your contract of employment and carry out regular appraisals to review your performance. If you do not achieve the level required then both you and your employer can take steps to deal with the problem. One solution may be to offer training. You may also agree a timetable for the necessary improvements to be made.

However, appraisals should also help to ensure that you get appropriate training and development of your skills. If a company is to benefit from employing you, it is in its interest to develop your skills.

Appraisals are normally carried out by your line manager or supervisor. They may be carried out every six or twelve months. When you start work in a company, you may have your first appraisal after three months. There are different ways of carrying out an appraisal, but it is important that both the employer and the employee have input into the process.

● ● ● Appraisal forms

Employers often use an appraisal form. It is used to record the discussion that takes place. It should include your name, job title, etc., the name of the person doing the appraisal, and the date of the next appraisal.

Your line manager may comment on items like attendance and timekeeping. You will be assessed on all or some of the following: overall performance, targets achieved, potential, strengths and weaknesses, communication skills, willingness to take on responsibility, time management, work management, willingness to exercise initiative, and ability to work without supervision.

The appraisal should include suggestions for training, and you should set targets and objectives. The form should be completed at the time of the discussion, and jointly agreed. The completed form will normally be kept on your personnel file.

Quality standards

The quality of the goods or services is vital to a company's reputation. One way of maintaining standards is to ensure that employees are kept up to date with any changes in the company, its structure, and its activities. This may be done through training.

• • • *Training schemes*

Companies spend time and money recruiting people and it is important that they develop this talent and improve the skill levels. One way of doing this is to encourage employees to participate in training. While personal development courses are always useful, employees often prefer to get additional qualifications. Training is often linked to recognised, external standards and qualifications. These might be specific to the company or industry, for example the National Vocational Qualifications.

Many companies also engage in the Investors in People scheme. A very large number of UK employers and employees have benefited from being involved in this scheme. It sets out a level of good practice for the training and development of people. Training and skills development are critical tools.

For schemes to work effectively, everyone in the organisation must:
• know and understand what is required of their job
• know how to do the job and why they are important
• have the necessary materials, tools, training and information to do the job well
• be able to measure how well they are doing
• know what to do when things go wrong
• work within systems and guidelines designed to help, not hinder
• be led and guided by managers.

• • • *The benefits of training schemes*

The organisation gets better results, better customer relations, and a motivated workforce. The customer gets better care, service, and confidence in the company. Employees get job satisfaction, a good working environment, recognition, and pride in being part of a successful company. They may see benefits such as:
• good quality training
• better communication
• skill and career development opportunities
• increased responsibility and involvement
• health and safety gains.

Investing in people can help companies to get accreditation for quality schemes such as ISO 9000. This is a quality standard that indicates that a company has well-documented processes, procedures and systems.

Assessment

Assessment establishes what standards of performance are within a company. The gap between what they are and what they need to be dictates the programme for improvement that is laid out in staff appraisals. Often assessments are carried out at the time of staff appraisals. There are companies that require employees to carry out self-assessment questionnaires every six months, or at the end of a project. However, if goods are being produced there will be continual quality checks on work – both by the worker and line managers. This is less likely if goods are not being produced.

Importance of standards

To keep customers happy a company must meet their needs. To do so *all* the people in the company have to do their job well and produce quality work. It is important that employees know what these standards are, and what is expected of them. It is only then that a company can provide consistent quality services.

The benefits of having standards include:
* skilled, motivated people work harder – this can result in improved productivity
* improved customer satisfaction
* high morale, improved retention rates, and less absenteeism.

▨▨▨ EVIDENCE ACTIVITIES

Monitoring work performance

1   How do employers monitor the work done by their employees?

2   Give three examples of how work procedures are used to monitor an individual's performance. For each example, you should include:
* who is involved in each procedure
* the responsibilities of each person involved.

Importance of monitoring

Why do you think it is important to monitor performance?

You should split your answer into three, by explaining the importance:

▷ to the employer

▷ to the employee

▷ to the customer.

Other procedures

• • • *Grievance procedure*

The purpose of this procedure is to provide an opportunity for any employee with a grievance to have it dealt with quickly and effectively. The procedure should outline the steps to be followed, such as:

1)   Put the grievance in writing to your line manager, who should resolve it within a specified time. If it is not dealt with within that time, the employee should be told why and when it will be. If the grievance involves the line manager, it should be raised with a more senior manager.

2) If the grievance is not resolved satisfactorily, it should then be raised with the next level of management, who should arrange to hear the grievance.

3) At a grievance interview the employee may be accompanied by a trade union official or a fellow employee. The response should be given within a specified time. If it is not dealt with within the time, the employee should be told why and when it will be.

• • • *Disciplinary procedure*

All employees should know what is considered to be a disciplinary offence and how it will be dealt with. Companies do not want to have unreasonable rules. Standards of behaviour are necessary for safety and order in the interest of all employees. It may be necessary to take action against employees whose behaviour, actions or performance are not acceptable.

If the action is not serious it may be dealt with informally. If this does not lead to improvement or if it is more serious, for example, continual absences, bad timekeeping, or poor performance, the grievance procedure will be used. A trade union official or fellow employee can be present during a disciplinary interview.

A disciplinary procedure will typically involve:

1) The employee will be given a formal *verbal warning*. They will be given the reason, and told that it is the first stage of the disciplinary procedure. A note of the verbal warning may be recorded.

2) If conduct or work performance does not improve, or if the action is more serious, a *first written warning* may be given. This will give details of the problem and what will happen if there is no improvement. This warning will be recorded.

3) If the employee does not improve, or repeats the action, or there is serious misconduct, it will result in a *final written warning*. This will give details of the problem and note that dismissal will probably result if there is no improvement. This warning will be recorded.

4) If you do not do what is required in a final written warning it will normally lead to *dismissal* with appropriate notice. The employee will be told why they are being dismissed and the date it will happen. If it is serious misconduct an employee may be suspended on full basic pay while an investigation is carried out.

Offences that are considered to amount to *gross misconduct* are so serious that an employee will normally be dismissed immediately. They include breaking the law, such as theft, or deliberately causing injury to another employee.

• • • *Health and Safety procedure*

You should be informed of the health and safety procedures, and the member of staff who is the health and safety representative. Your employer has a duty to ensure that you have a safe environment in which to work.

> ### GIVE IT A GO disciplinary and grievance procedure
>
> 1   What can your employer do if you are continually late for work?
> 2   What can you do if:
> * One of your colleagues seems to be drinking alcohol at work?
> * You keep getting headaches because it is dark in the office in which you work?
> * After two years in your job, you are the only one who has not yet had any additional skills training?

unit 3

Developing skills in IT

This unit has been designed to give you the opportunity to use the basic functions of a computer and its operating system. You will look at the desktop facilities and how to organise files. You will learn how to control and operate windows. You will also learn how to use the computer and printer.

In this unit you will need to learn about:

▷ a computer's desktop settings

▷ how to work in a windows environment with icons and desktop applications

▷ how to store data in a computer

▷ standard ways of working.

Desktop settings

Features for running a computer

• • • *PC components*

We will start by investigating the different components of a PC (Personal Computer). (Note that this is covered in even greater depth in Unit 7.)

A PC processes data by following instructions. It is made up of:

Hardware

This means all the physical devices, including:

- *The monitor*: This is also known as the VDU (Visual Display Unit). It allows you to view not only what you are carrying out on the PC but also the results of the work carried out by the processor.
- *The keyboard*: This is one of the input devices (a means by which you can begin the instructions). It consists of keys based on the standard typewriter layout, 'QWERTY', plus additional keys, such as: function keys, arrow keys, the Control (**Ctrl**), **Alt** and **Shift** keys.
- *The mouse*: This is another input device – it is a pointing device that enables you to select and move items on the screen. The buttons on the mouse can be used to select options. Movements are tracked by sensors in its base. The mouse pointer is displayed in differing ways depending on position and function. Here are the commonly-used **mouse terms**:

TERM	ACTION
Click	Press and release the mouse button.
Double-click	Quickly press and release the mouse button twice.
Drag and drop	When the mouse pointer is over an object on your screen, press and hold down the left mouse button. Still holding down the button, move to where you want to replace the object. Release the mouse button.
Hover	Place the mouse pointer over an object for a few seconds so that something happens – e.g. another menu appears, or a Tooltip.

- *The processor*: This is the means by which the instructions (or programs) are carried out. There are different types of processor – e.g. Pentium. The speed at which they perform is measured in megahertz (MHz).

A flatscreen monitor and keyboard

- *The printer*: This is one of the output devices for a computer. It is a means by which you can view your work as hard copy.

Software

This means the programs (series of instructions) running on the hardware. The programs that run the PC are called system software. Windows is an operating system that ensures that all parts of the computer system work together. It controls the hardware and starts and operates the software. It provides ways to manage files stored on the computer.

Packages such as word processors, spreadsheets, databases and drawing programs are all examples of applications software.

Memory

This means the place where instructions and data are stored. A computer has two types of memory:

- *RAM*: Random Access Memory is the short-term memory. Power is required to retain information, and data stored in RAM is lost when power is turned off. The greater the capacity the PC has to temporarily store instructions and data, the quicker programs will run. RAM is faster than ROM.
- *ROM*: Read Only Memory permanently stores instructions and data.

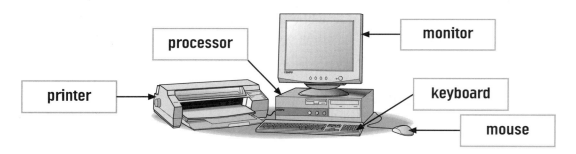

Figure 3.1 Components of a PC system

••• *Starting your system*

When your PC components have been connected together, you can switch on your PC. The operating system will be loaded and the opening screen will be displayed (Figure 3.2). The system used in the examples uses Windows XP and Office XP. Your screens will look different if you are using other software.

••• *Starting an application or program*

Before you can carry out any work on your PC you must first load the program or application. From the **start** menu, select **All Programs**. When the menu displaying the programs available on your system is displayed, select the application you wish to use (Figure 3.3).

**Figure 3.2
Opening
screen**

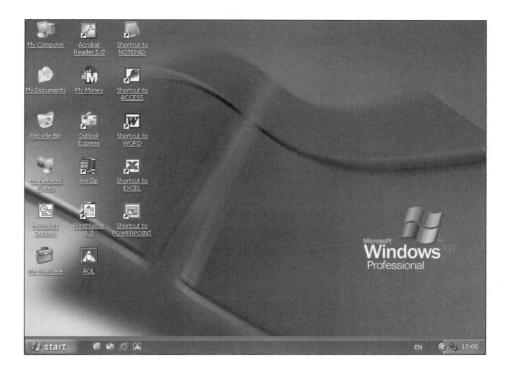

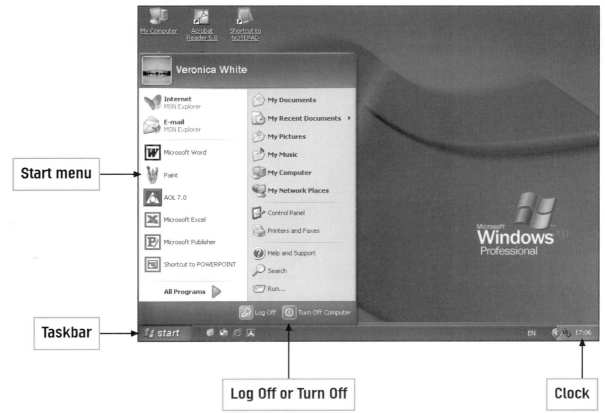

Figure 3.3   Starting an application

GIVE IT A GO getting started

Switch on your system and make sure that it is all ready for use.

1 From your opening screen, click on the **All Programs** button to display the programs available.

2 Select and load **Word**.

3 Close the application without saving (by going to the **Close** button at the top right corner of the screen).

• • • *Getting on-line help*

You can get Windows Help by clicking on the **start** button, then on **Help and Support**. The **Help and Support Center** window will be displayed (Figure 3.4).

In the Search box, key in the name of the topic you are looking for

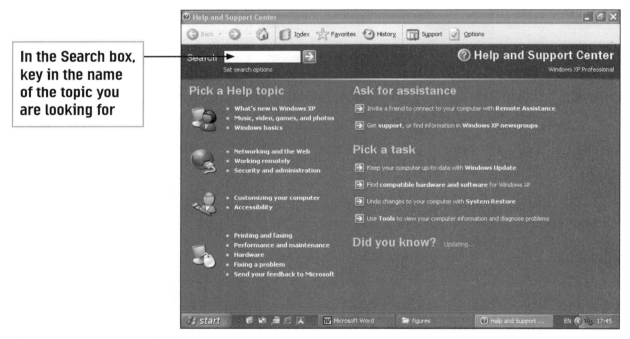

Figure 3.4 Windows Help

• • • *Shutting down or re-booting your system*

When you have finished working on your computer, you may want to shut it down. You should ideally not just switch off the power. You should first ensure that you have saved any files you have been working on, and closed down any applications that may still be running.

Finally, go to the start menu, and select **Turn off computer**. You will be given the option to hibernate (save your current desktop state so you can resume where you left off), turn off the computer or to re-boot (**Restart**). You may want to re-boot if you have changed an important setting, loaded a new application, or simply if the computer is 'freezing' or has developed other temporary problems.

■■■ EVIDENCE ACTIVITY

PC components and their basic functions

1   Label the components of the PC system in the diagram above.

2   Explain what each of the components does, and why you need them.

3   Check that all the components on your system are connected.

4   Switch on your PC.

5   Produce a screen shot (see Introduction page XX to learn how this is done) and identify:
   • the start menu
   • the taskbar
   • the clock
   • the shutdown button.

6   What is RAM?

7   Explain how to get on-line help.

Desktop configuration

This term describes how your PC looks on screen and works. You can use the **Control Panel** to view and, if you wish, alter the default settings. Access the **Control Panel** by selecting it from the **start** button. You will then be able to decide how your computer works and looks. You can also add or remove software (programs), hardware (such as printers or scanners), and set up network connections and user accounts (Figures 3.5 and 3.6).

Figure 3.5 The Control Panel – Classic View

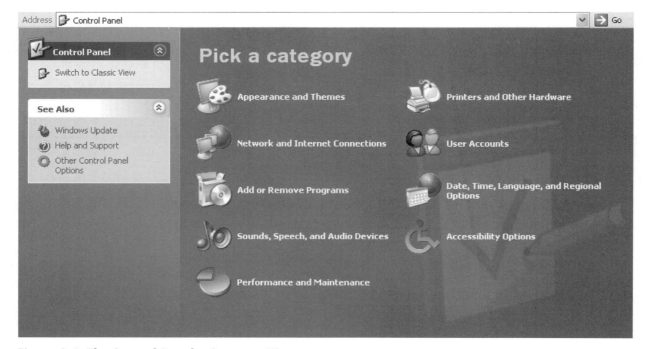

Figure 3.6 The Control Panel – Category View

• • • *Control Panel icons*

Here are some of the Control Panel icons for basic functions, and their descriptions:

 To adjust settings for vision, hearing and mobility

 To set the date, time and time zone

 To change the appearance of the desktop – such as background, screen saver, colours, font sizes and screen resolution

 To alter the keyboard settings such as cursor blink rate and character repeat rate

 To customise the mouse settings such as button configuration, double-click speed, mouse pointers and motion speed

 To configure energy saving settings

 To customise settings for the display of languages, numbers, times and dates

 To view information about your computer system and change settings for hardware, performance, and automatic updates

 To customise the Start menu and the taskbar – such as the types of items to be displayed and how they will appear

 To change user account settings and passwords for people who share the computer

• • • *Changing the desktop configuration*

To change any aspect of your desktop configuration, double-click on your chosen icon, and select from the options you see. As an example, to change the date and time on your computer:

1) Double-click on the **Date and Time** icon. When the **Date and Time Properties** dialogue box is displayed check the details (Figure 3.7). Click in the relevant boxes to change the date and time if necessary.

2) If you make any changes, click on **Apply** and then on **OK** to close the box.

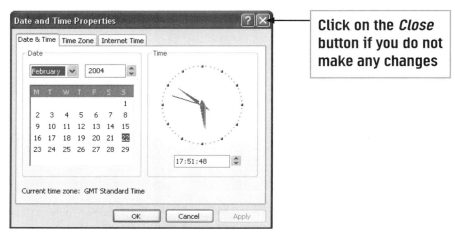

> Click on the *Close* button if you do not make any changes

Figure 3.7 Date and Time Properties dialogue box

GIVE IT A GO   explore desktop configuration

Look at each of the icons shown on page 37. Do **not** make any changes to the settings. Make notes regarding the options you look at, for example do you like a particular screen saver? Take time to investigate all the options available.

▨▨▨ EVIDENCE ACTIVITY

Desktop settings

1   Go to the **Display** icon on the **Control Panel**. Before you begin make a note of the current settings for the **theme**.

2   Change the **theme** to **Jungle**.

3   Produce a simple document for a new user describing:
   • the general procedure for changing desktop settings
   • how to change the desktop display theme.

Text and dialogue boxes

Dialogue boxes are displayed on screen if you wish to carry out a function. They are a means of giving instructions to complete a procedure if there is more than one option, or if you have to enter information (Figure 3.8).

The name of the dialogue box is shown in the top left corner of the box

The Close button

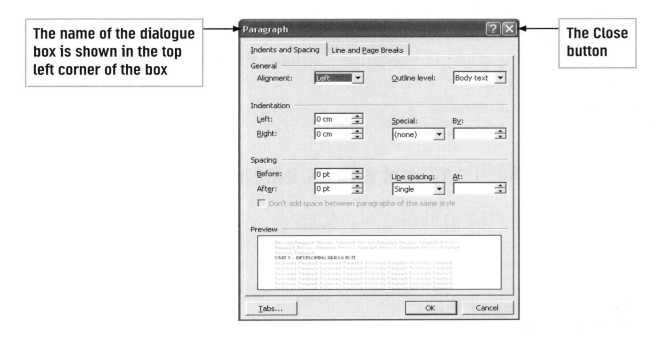

Figure 3.8 The Paragraph dialogue box

If a text box shows the symbol shown in Figure 3.9 in the corner you can not only move the box but also re-size it by placing the mouse on the corner marker and either moving in to make it smaller or pulling out to make it bigger. You can also change the width or the height by using the side, top or bottom edges of the box.

Figure 3.9 Changing the size of a dialogue box

When you have selected the options you require, or entered any necessary information, you complete the procedure by clicking on **OK**.

To move a dialogue box go to the top of the box and holding down the mouse move the box to the required position.

To select from a drop-down list move the band to the required option and click (Figure 3.10).

Figure 3.10 Selecting from a drop–down list

■■● EVIDENCE ACTIVITY

Dialogue boxes

1   Open **Word**, and a new document (select **New** from the **File** menu).

2   Open the **Insert File** dialogue box by selecting **File** from the **Insert** menu.

3   Re-size the dialogue box to be as small as possible.

4   Move the dialogue box to the top right of the screen.

5   Provide a screen shot as evidence that you have carried out this procedure.

6   Close the dialogue box.

7   Close the document without saving.

■ ■ ■ ■ Windows environment

Working with program windows

To start a program go to the **start** button, then highlight **All Programs**. The programs that are available will be displayed on your screen (Figure 3.11):

Figure 3.11 The All Programs menu

Once you have selected the program icon you want to use, a new program window will come up on screen.

At the top of your screen you will see boxes that allow you to minimise, maximise and close that window (Figure 3.12).

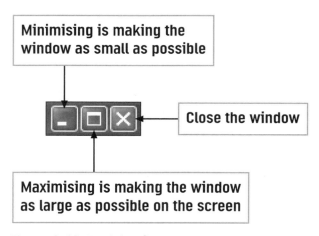

Minimising is making the window as small as possible

Close the window

Maximising is making the window as large as possible on the screen

Figure 3.12 Resizing buttons

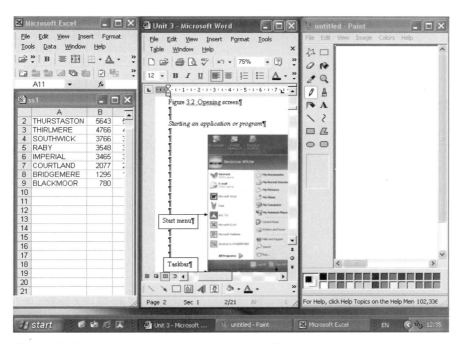

Resizing a window allows you to view more than one program open and visible on the screen. To resize a window, place the cursor at the side, or in the corner place holder, and move inwards until it is the required size. See Figure 3.12. Figure 3.13 shows Word, Excel and Paint all open and displayed.

Figure 3.13 Displaying more than one application program

Icons

Icons are small images or pictures. They are a quick method of allowing you to carry out a function, such as inserting a hyperlink, making text bold or italic, or printing. *Shortcut* icons are a quick method of loading application programs.

If you are not sure what an icon does, hover the mouse over it. Text will appear to give a description of the function. The main types of icon that you see on a normal Desktop are:

Application or **Program** shortcut icons such as Notepad, Access, Word, Excel and PowerPoint, shown below:

File icons (with details of type and size shown):

Folder icons that look like this:

module 4

▓▓▓ EVIDENCE ACTIVITIES

Icons

1 Click on the **My Computer** icon on your desktop.

2 Describe what this facility is for.

3 Click on the **Recycle bin** icon on your desktop.

4 Describe what this facility is for.

Shortcut icons

1 What is a shortcut icon?

2 Are there any shortcut icons on your desktop?

3 What is their purpose?

Desktop application parts

When you load a desktop application you will be able to see the following items:

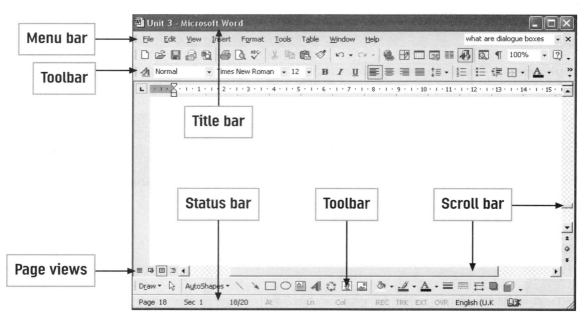

Figure 3.14 Desktop application parts

ITEM	FUNCTION
Title bar	This shows the name of the file and the application you are using.
Menu bar	This shows the functions available for use. When you select any of these functions, a drop-down menu will appear giving you further options.
Toolbar	This shows icons which are a quick method of carrying out (usually the most common) functions available on the menu bar. You can display different toolbars as you wish. It is possible to turn them on and off.
Scroll bars	When a window is not big enough to display all the information in it, scroll bars appear – vertically and/or horizontally. They allow you to move up and down or across.
Status bar	This shows your position in a document as well as items such as whether you are in Overwrite mode.
Page views	Most application programs allow you to view your current work in a number of ways. For example, Word allows Normal, Web Layout, Print Layout and Outline views. You will select the most appropriate for the work you are carrying out.
Task bar	This is not part of an application window, but it is always on screen whatever else you are doing (see page 33, Figure 3.3). It displays the name of each open window allowing you to switch easily between applications or individual documents.

GIVE IT A GO displaying toolbars

Load **Word**. From the **View** menu, under **Toolbars**, see what happens when you select from the list of toolbars. You can switch off ones that are already on, and vice versa – but only one at a time. Each time you select, you have to return to the **Toolbars** menu to change the settings again.

WHAT if

1   What would you do if a toolbar you required was not displayed?
2   What would you do if an icon you wanted to use was not displayed on a toolbar?
3   Why would you choose not to display toolbars?
4   How do you identify whether a toolbar is displayed on the View menu?

■■■ EVIDENCE ACTIVITY

Desktop application parts

1 Load **Word** and make a screen print (see page ix of the Introduction for instructions on how this is done).

2 Label the screen print with these desktop application parts:

title bar	menu bar	toolbars
page views	status bar	scroll bars

3 Explain the purpose of each of the items.

    # Store data in a computer

Drives

• • • *The hard drive*

This is used to store the system files, application files and any files and folders that you create on your PC. Most PCs have a hard (fixed) disk drive installed – (usually) inside the computer. Hard disks provide faster retrieval of information compared with floppy disks. Hard disk capacity is large, and so it is measured in MB (Megabytes) or GB (Gigabytes). It is most frequently named as the **C:** drive.

• • • *The floppy drive*

This is not used as much today. The disks are smaller and removable, and are often used to store backups of your work from your PC. It is most frequently named as the **A:** drive. Floppy disks vary in the amount of space they have available on them. Many disks are now formatted when you buy them but if not, you will need to format (or prepare) the disk for use on your computer.

The 3.5 inch floppy disk has become the norm. It provides a cheap way of backing up small amounts of data. It has a hard plastic case (protecting the floppy interior) with a metal cover which slides back when the disk is placed in the disk drive. The amount that can be stored on a floppy disk depends on whether it is single or double sided, and whether it is single, double or high density.

GIVE IT A GO | memory capacity

Memory capacity describes the amount of space on a disk onto which you can save your files.

Find out the memory capacity of:

▷ the hard drive on your system

▷ a floppy disk that can be used on your system.

WHAT if

1   A floppy disk you have saved your work on does not allow you to re-load that work. What would you do?

2   A new floppy disk does not work on your system. What procedure would you have to carry out so that you can use it?

Floppy disks have a notch, called the write-protect notch, which will stop you from deleting or altering the contents of that disk. On 3.5 inch disks there is a small tab in one corner that slides across to write-protect it.

To ensure floppy disks are not damaged, you should do the following:
• Do not touch the exposed recording surface.
• Keep the disks away from anything magnetic.
• Keep the disks away from direct heat such as radiators or sunlight.
• Store the disks carefully.

• • • *The CD-ROM drive*

This is now commonplace for PCs. A CD-ROM is a round, flat optical device. A narrow, fast laser beam is used to read the data which has been etched onto the surface. Retrieval is fast. As the size of the software programs has increased, it is now usually distributed on CD-ROMs rather than floppy disks.

A CD can hold in excess of 600MB, equivalent to 500 floppy disks. Usually used in the **D:** drive, these types are available:
• CD-R   a recordable CD that can be written to once only
• CD-RW   recordable and can be used many times
• CD-WORM   Write Once Read Many – allows the user to write data once only.

• • • *Structure of drives*

Folders (or directories) are the method by which all documents with the same theme are kept together. **Sub-folders** are other folders in a main folder. The root folder or directory is the first place you select in order to find a file or application.

The easiest way to visualise the structure of the drives on your computer is to look at Windows Explorer. This is a kind of contents index of everything on your computer. To reach it, select **start**, **All Programs**, **Accessories**, **Windows Explorer**. The structure of files and folders is shown on the left. When you click on a folder it branches out to show its contents as a list. A different, more expanded view of the contents is shown on the right.

An electronic notebook with a CD–ROM partially inserted

■■■ EVIDENCE ACTIVITIES

Structure of drives

Create a diagram showing a folder for your files for this course. Label the parts like this:

1   Name the folder **BTEC.**

2   There should be three sub-folders named **UNIT-1, UNIT-2** and **UNIT-3.**

3   In each of these sub-folders put two further sub-folders named **SOURCE** and **ANSWERS.**

4   In the sub-folder **ANSWERS** place the files **U3S1** and **CAPACITY.**

Properties of drives

1   What letter is the hard disk drive usually allocated?

2   What letter is the floppy disk drive usually allocated?

3   What letter is the CD-ROM drive usually allocated?

4   Why should you take care of floppy disks and CD-ROMs?

5   What factors should you consider when purchasing removable disks, and why?

Properties of folders and files

The *properties* of folders and files include:

• • • *Name*

You can name files and folders using any name that you choose, as long as it is unique. However, you will have to take into consideration any conventions used in the environment in which you work. It is also possible to change (or **rename**) the name of any file or folder that you have created.

• • • *Size*

The size of a file will depend on the amount of text or data that you put into it. It is important to know the file size if you wish to copy it (say to a floppy or CD) to decide if there is sufficient space to accept a file of that size.

• • • *Date last updated*

The date you last worked on a file or in a folder is automatically recorded by the operating system, and becomes part of the properties of that file or folder. It can be a useful feature if you are searching for a file and have forgotten the name.

• • • *Type*

When you save a file, the computer automatically gives it an extension depending on the application in which you are working, for example, the **.doc** extension denotes that it is a **Word** file. Other common file extensions are:

.xls	Excel	.mdb	Access
.ppt	PowerPoint	.bmp	Paint
.txt	Notepad	.htm	HTML files used on the World Wide Web
.rtf	Rich Text Format – this is readable by most of the common word processor applications		

● ● ● *Viewing file properties*

To view the properties of a file, highlight the file and right-click on the mouse.
Select **Properties** from the menu.

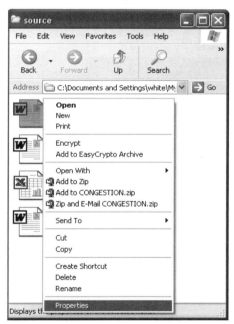

Figure 3.15 Selecting Properties

When the Properties dialogue box is displayed you will see the file name in the top
left corner. There are three tabs:

General	This gives outline details of the file including the file type, size and when it was created.
Custom	This allows you to create any new property field you wish to add.
Summary	**Simple** – This shows the title, subject and author.
	Advanced – This shows further information including number of pages, word count, character count, and line count. It also includes the revision number, application name, company, date created, date last saved, edit time.

These figures show the various tabs on the Properties dialogue box:

Figure 3.16 General tab

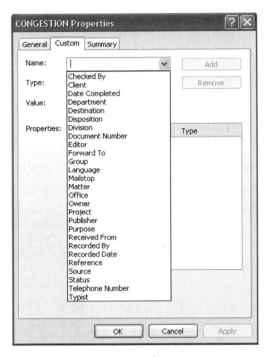

Figure 3.17 Custom tab

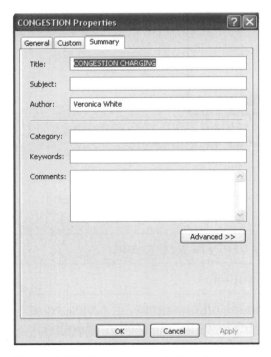

Figure 3.18 Summary tab Simple

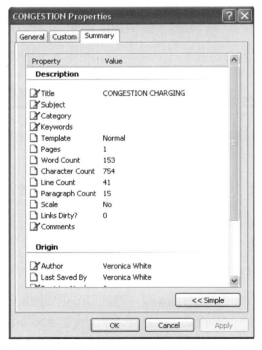

Figure 3.19 Summary tab Advanced

You can also use the toolbar buttons to view file properties. Click on the down arrow at the end of the **Views** icon and select **Details** to view the file details in a list.

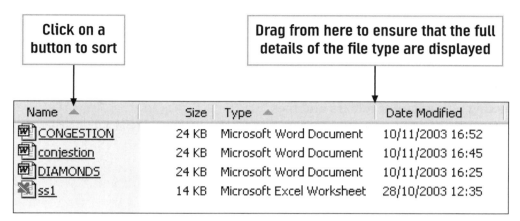

Click on a button to sort

Drag from here to ensure that the full details of the file type are displayed

Name ▲	Size	Type ▲	Date Modified
CONGESTION	24 KB	Microsoft Word Document	10/11/2003 16:52
conjestion	24 KB	Microsoft Word Document	10/11/2003 16:45
DIAMONDS	24 KB	Microsoft Word Document	10/11/2003 16:25
ss1	14 KB	Microsoft Excel Worksheet	28/10/2003 12:35

Figure 3.20 File properties shown in Details format

Clicking on the button at the top of any section will sort the details. You can sort by Name, Size, Type or Date. In the example above, the files are sorted into ascending order of Type. If the information is not displayed in full, drag the border as indicated.

GIVE IT A GO   file properties

Write down the properties of three files on your computer. Make sure that they are different file types. Present them in this way:

PROPERTY	FILE 1	FILE 2	FILE 3
Name			
Size			
Type			
Location			
Date created			
Date modified			

File functions

• • • *Selecting folders and files*

Selecting individual folders and files

To select an individual file or folder go to it and highlight it.

Selecting adjacent folders and files

To select more than one file select the first folder or file in the group. Hold down the **Shift** key on the keyboard and select the last file you require.

Selecting non-adjacent folders and files

Select the first folder or file. Hold down the **Ctrl** key on the keyboard and select each file you require.

• • • *Copying folders and files*

There are a number of ways to copy a file:

1) Locate the folders you will copy from and to. Select the file you will copy and hold down the *left* mouse button on it. At the same time, hold down the **Ctrl** key. Drag the file to the folder into which you want the copy to be placed. Release the **Ctrl** key and the mouse button.

2) Select the folders you will copy from and to. Select the file you want to copy. Hold down the *right* mouse button and drag the file to the folder to which it is to be copied. Release the mouse. When the menu is displayed click on **Copy here**.

3) Right-click on the file you want to copy. When the menu is displayed select **Copy**. Right-click on the folder to which the file is to be copied, and then select **Paste**.

4) Select the folder you will copy the file from and highlight the file to be copied. A menu (**File and Folder tasks**) will be displayed on the left of the screen. Select **Copy this file**. The **Copy Items** dialogue box will be displayed. Select the location to which the file will be copied, and then click on: **Copy**.

(Methods 3 and 4 are easiest when you have numerous files and folders, as they may scroll out of view when you are trying to drag them (methods 1 and 2). Folders can be copied in the same way.

• • • *Moving folders and files*

Files and folders can be moved following the methods above, except in:

1) Do not hold down the **Ctrl** key when moving files or folders.
2) Select **Move here** instead of **Copy Here**.
3) Select **Cut** instead of **Copy**.
4) Select **Move this File** instead of **Copy this File**.

• • • *Renaming or deleting a file or folder*

Renaming a file or folder

First select the file or folder and right-click on it. Select **Rename** from the pop-up menu, and key in the new name. Press: **Enter**.

Deleting a file or folder

First select the file or folder. Press the **Delete** key. When you are asked to confirm the deletion click on **Yes**.

• • • *Creating a folder*

How to do this is illustrated in Unit 9, page 154. An alternative to the methods there, is: right-click in the location that you want the folder to be created. A menu will come up. Select **New**, and then **Folder**. Enter the name for the new folder.

• • • *Moving between open windows*

When you are working you may find that you have more than one window open. The open windows will appear (minimised) on the taskbar. To switch between windows click on the button for the window that you want displayed.

• • • *Using a 'find' tool – searching*

To find a file or folder:

1) From the **start** menu, click on **Search**.
2) The **Search Results** dialogue box is displayed.
3) Click on the arrow next to **All files and folders**.
4) In the **All or part of the file name** box, key in the name of the file you want to find.
5) Enter any other details you may know to assist in the search.
6) Click on the **Search** button.

Any files or folders meeting the criteria will be placed on the right-hand pane.

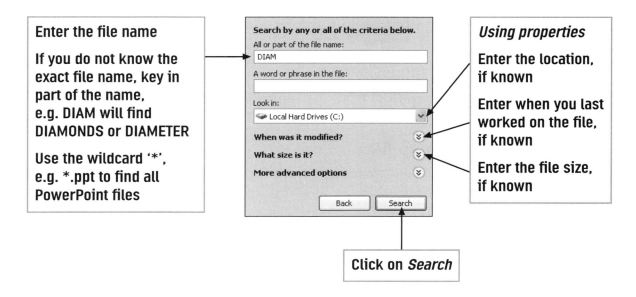

Figure 3.21 Searching for files or folders

■■■ EVIDENCE ACTIVITY

Manipulating files and folders

On your computer, create the folder structure you drew up for the *Structure of drives* exercise (page 46). Do this in a suitable part of the computer, such as within your own work area — your tutor will advise you. Your tutor will also tell you where to get the files **U3S1** and **CAPACITY**.

● ● ● *Saving*

To save a file you are working on you can click on the **Save** icon on the toolbar OR click on **Save As** from the **File** menu.

You can then select the location in the **Save in** box to:

*   the hard disk (C:)
*   the floppy disk (A:)
*   the CD (D:).

To save as a different file type, select the type you require from the drop-down menu at the end of the **Save as type** box.

**Figure 3.22
The Save As
dialogue box**

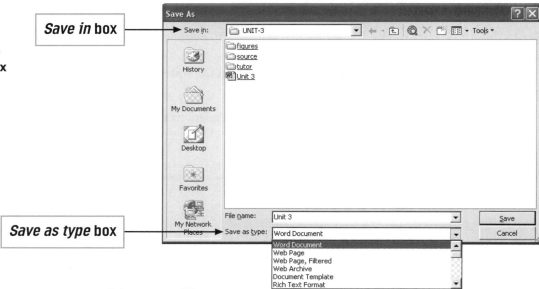

● ● ● *Backing up files*

Backing up a disk means producing an exact copy of the contents of the disk. This is done as a security measure in case anything happens to the original disk.

First select your floppy disk drive. Right-click and a menu will be displayed. Select **Copy disk** and follow the instructions on screen.

You can also backup your data from your hard drive by selecting **Programs, Accessories, System Tools, Backup** from the **start** menu, and then following the instructions given. If you want to backup selected files only, copy them to CD or to floppy disk by the usual copying or saving procedures (see above).

Understand the standard ways of working

Standard procedures for security

The security you put in place on your system will protect it from misuse. It can include:

• • • *Logging on and off*

You should use the correct procedures and rules for logging on and particularly for logging off. Ensure that all programs and files are closed down before switching off or damage may be caused to them and your system.

• • • *Using passwords*

You should use passwords to secure your working area and files from misuse. In some cases several passwords are needed to access strictly confidential data to provide additional security. Files can also be password protected. Use a password that is not easy for anyone to guess and do not give your password to anyone.

• • • *Virus checking*

You should virus check any files you are loading onto your computer. This will protect your computer from being infected by programs that can cause damage to the system and your files. A computer virus is a destructive program within a program, written by people wanting to cause problems for computer users.

• • • *Backing up files*

This means that you should make copies of files on your computer. You will normally have a copy of the system software, and the backups that you will make will be of any files you create. You can use removable disks or tapes. You should store backups in a safe place away from your computer.

⬛⬛⬛ EVIDENCE ACTIVITIES

Security procedures
Draw up instructions for a new user using your system for:

▷ logging on and logging off

▷ the use of passwords — include guidance on selecting passwords and frequency of changing them.

Importance of security

1 Explain why it is important to use virus checking software.

2 Develop a (simple) backup procedure, explaining why you have made your decisions. Include the frequency, storage, etc.

3 Your system crashes. What would need to be done to recover the system?

Legislation

There is important legislation that applies to the use of computers and to the environment in which you work, which means there are rules you must follow. They include the Computer Misuse Act, the Data Protection Act and the Health and Safety at Work Act.

• • • *Data Protection Act 1998*

First passed in the UK in 1984, it was updated in 1998 and the changes came into effect on 1 March 2000. It sets out rules for use of personal information not only on computers, but also on some paper records. It allows individuals the right to know what information is held about them.

There are exceptions – the police, and sometimes medical records.

Anyone holding computerised data on individuals must register with the Data Protection Registrar as a data user. There are eight principles to ensure that information is handled properly. The data must be:

- fairly and lawfully processed
- processed for limited purposes
- adequate, relevant and not excessive
- accurate
- not kept for longer than necessary
- processed in line with your rights
- secure
- not transferred to other countries without adequate protection.

• • • *Health and Safety at Work etc Act 1974*

This legislation, administered by the Health and Safety Executive, covers IT environments. It is vital that the equipment is safe. Power cables should be secured so that they cannot be tripped over and power sockets should not be overloaded.

Your workspace should be comfortable, or you may become tired, ill or injured. Repetitive strain injury (RSI) is any injury arising from making awkward movements or by the prolonged use of particular muscles. It can affect the back, arms and hands, neck, and eyes.

It is important to take frequent breaks and rest your eyes by focusing them on something in the distance and walking around.

• • • *Computer Misuse Act 1990*

This act makes it illegal to gain unauthorised access or make unauthorised modification of computer material. Either the person or the computer has to be in the home country when the unauthorised action is carried out. It is an offence to attempt:

- *Unauthorised access to computer material*: It is an offence to perform any function on a computer to gain unauthorised access to any program or data.
- *Unauthorised access with intent to commit or facilitate commission of further offences*: It does not matter if a further offence is to be committed on the same occasion as the unauthorised access or in the future, even if that turns out to be impossible.
- *Unauthorised modification of computer material*: It is an offence to try to cause an unauthorised modification of the contents of a computer, or to impair the operation of the computer by a modification, i.e. to prevent access to a program or data, to stop a program from running, or to affect the reliability of data. This is the case for any computer, any program or any data. It does not matter whether the change (and any effect) is permanent or temporary.

▣▣▣ EVIDENCE ACTIVITIES

Data protection

1   Can you change another user's password without their permission?

2   What would you do if one of your colleagues changed the data on the personnel files so that it appeared that you had all worked more hours last month?

3   Draw up a list of the Dos and Don'ts for a person answering the telephone regarding queries from the general public.

IT skills presentation

1   Prepare a short verbal presentation for a group of 10- to 11-year-old beginners to explain:
   - PC components
   - Desktop features
   - Icons and window parts, e.g. sizing and toolbars
   - Folders, files and storage
   - Security and legislation.

2   You should provide audience notes and/or handouts.

You may use a presentation program to help you. You will find guidelines for preparing and delivering presentations in Unit 9 page 165.

unit 4

4

Personal effectiveness

This unit has been designed to allow you the chance of exploring your own potential by looking at your skills in relation to the IT job market. You will investigate the requirements of specific jobs and match your strengths against them. You can look at the range of personality and psychometric testing available. You will create your own CV.

In this unit you will need to learn about:

▷ how to carry out a personal audit to help find suitable jobs

▷ how to explore your potential in relation to suitable jobs

▷ how to prepare a personal statement and portfolio for employment.

Personal audit

The first thing that you need to do is to look at the skills that you already have, and start to build up a portfolio. This should include:

Vocational skills

Gather together information regarding any work-related experience. Include any part-time jobs, work experience, or voluntary work that you have carried out. You should think about what was involved in each of them.

- What skills did you need to do the job?
- What did you like about the job?
- What did you dislike about the job?

You should also gather together any practical qualifications you have achieved including any first aid experience and certificates, swimming or life-saving certificates or Duke of Edinburgh awards.

Personal skills

How do you like to present yourself?

• • • *Appearance*

Appearance is an important factor in employment. Do you like to dress formally or casually? When you think about being in a job, do you see yourself in a uniform? What do you think your appearance might tell a prospective employer? What do other people say about how you dress?

• • • *Body language*

Body language also has an impact on the way you are perceived. It is important to create a confident first impression to achieve credibility. How you stand, sit, walk and use gestures can have either a positive or a negative effect. Non-verbal communication, such as smiling, can also contribute to your presentation.

• • • *Key characteristics*

You may want to think about some of the people who you admire. Many of them have things in common – key characteristics – which are things that make people effective, including:

- knowing their goals – and if the first approach does not work, trying another
- being proactive – taking the lead rather than waiting for things to happen
- leading by example – influencing others and bringing together people with different values
- prioritising and working out strategies so that no one has to be the loser
- carrying out all necessary jobs while continuing to expand the mind with new ideas.

Interpersonal skills

How do you get on with other people? Are you quiet, strident, calm? Do other people seek your advice? Is getting on with people important to you, or would you prefer to be alone?

Whatever your choice in your personal life, at work you will have to relate to others. If you find this difficult you should try to improve your skills. This will help you to become more confident about dealing with customers and colleagues.

Behaviour

Most companies have a code of conduct that outlines how the company expects its employees to conduct themselves. The company tries to cover all situations. If you are unsure about how to act or behave, you should ask for advice. Remember that you will be expected to act in a sensible, responsible manner. This is a brief look at some of the items that may be included in a Code of Conduct for Employees:

- *Employees making unauthorised communications may render themselves liable to disciplinary action.*

- *Employees should exercise care not to disclose commercially sensitive information.*

- *All employees should be clear about their contractual obligations and should not take outside employment which conflicts with company interests.*

- *No outside work of any sort should be undertaken in the office, and use of facilities, e.g. telephones, or access to computer facilities for outside work, is forbidden.*

- *There is a general expectation that dress will be appropriate to the standards set by individual departments. Individual departments will introduce an appropriate dress code to suit the services they provide and to meet the expectations of customers.*

Interests

Your interests can tell people a lot about the kind of person you are. Be honest about your interests. Do not be tempted to put down things that you think make you sound more interesting. For example, do not put down regular theatre visits if this is not true – the interviewer may know a lot about the theatre!

GIVE IT A GO   common interests

Select three of the common interests shown below:

animals	plants	drawing	talking	music	film
theatre	travel	sports	museums	history	dancing

Outline what you think you need to do to develop each interest effectively.

Transferable skills

These are skills you have acquired through any jobs, volunteer work, hobbies, sports, or other life experiences that can be used in your job. Listing interests on a CV is more useful if you think about what they have taught you. You should think about the qualities that are required to participate in them. Here are some examples:

- If you are a keen runner you have to work hard to improve your time – you can focus on a task.
- The fact that you take part in sport indicates that you are competitive – which is important in some jobs.
- If a company were looking for life skills, a person who had travelled independently might impress.
- If a company were looking for leadership, having been captain of a team, such as a chess team or sports team would be relevant.

▦▦▦ EVIDENCE ACTIVITY

Identify your job-related skills

1   List the five things you value most in life and rank them in order of importance.

2   What are the three most important goals in your life? Write down whatever comes to mind first — take only about half a minute.

3   What do you most enjoy doing?

4   What gives you the greatest personal satisfaction?

5   What would you attempt if you knew you could **not** fail?

6   Imagine your ideal future — what do you see? Use these points to help you.

- In my ideal future, I am ....

- I spend my days...

- I live ....

- I never...

- I have learned to ....

- My friends say that I am ....

- I have overcome...

- I am able to...

- When I think about what my life has become, I feel ....

7   What do your answers tell you about where you are now and where you would like to be in the future?

8   Do you think you need to make any changes to your current way of life?

 **Potential**

Assessment

Self-assessment is about gathering information about your values, interests, personality, and skills. You should bear in mind that we often see ourselves in a different light to the way others see us. Self-assessment and assessment by others of your values, personality and skills may paint a different picture.

• • • *Values*

These are the things that are important to you, like achievement, status, and control. Your values are possibly the most important factor to consider – if you do not there is a good chance you will not like your work and therefore not succeed in it. For example, someone who needs to have choice at work would not be happy in a job where every action is decided by someone else.

You should ask yourself questions like – Is a high salary important? Do you want a job where you interact with people? Does your work have to make a contribution to society? Is having a prestigious job important for you?

• • • *Interests*

These are your likes and dislikes – such as reading, running, sports and music.

• • • *Personality*

A personality assessment looks at your character, motivation, needs, and attitudes. We are all different and the things that motivate us are different. We have different needs. Fulfilling these needs can make us happier – but you need to know what they are, and think about jobs that meet these needs.

What makes you tick? Is it money, position, power, attention or responsibility? You may want to be accepted, independent or appreciated. You may want to have stability, power, influence or control.

• • • *Personality profiles*

People of a particular personality type are better suited to certain careers. Many studies have been carried out, including some on IT professionals. Here are some conclusions of the studies, about the type of personality typically found in certain IT jobs:

Software development
This field, which includes learning programming languages such as Visual Basic and C++, is attractive to people who are patient, logical thinkers who can work with abstract concepts. They are usually good at maths and are somewhat introverted. You may find them doing crossword puzzles, playing individual sports such as tennis or golf and engaged in strategy or role-playing games.

Networking

This field, which includes an in-depth knowledge of operating systems such as Windows NT and UNIX, appeals to an outgoing person who enjoys working with people. They enjoy working with their hands and prefer having a number of different assignments in different places. You will often find them building or fixing things and playing team sports such as football or cricket.

Database management

This field, which includes such products as Oracle and Microsoft SQL Server, suits people who love detail and are extremely organised. They tend to be somewhat introverted. They think in a holistic (whole picture) manner. You will often find them involved in activities similar to software developers.

Although profiles are generalisations, certain characteristics exist within groups. You need to find the IT field that best suits you, but remember that not all people in software development are introverts, and not all people involved in networking are extroverts.

More companies are now using personality questionnaires. If you are asked to take one of these, bear in mind that there are no right or wrong answers. Instead, a picture emerges of how you like to work. For example, do you like being organised, working with other people, or working alone?

● ● ● *Skills*

These are what you are good at – such as writing, programming or public speaking. A skills assessment also helps you realise what you enjoy doing. The skills you use in your career should combine both. You can use the results to acquire or develop skills that you need for a particular career.

When assessing your skills, you should consider the time you are willing to spend on acquiring more advanced or new skills. Ask yourself – if a career has everything I want but it takes five years to prepare for it, am I willing and able to make this time commitment?

Identify strengths and weaknesses

Whatever your strengths and weaknesses are, you need to identify them. You should then cross check your assessment with the opinion that others have of you. This will give you the opportunity to amend your list, if necessary, and also to work on the weaknesses that may be highlighted.

● ● ● *Strengths*

You may have the ability to listen and ask appropriate questions, follow instructions or get on well with other people (customers and colleagues). You may have strong administrative abilities and be a good organiser. You may be good at using your initiative or adaptable in learning new skills. You may be confident.

● ● ● *Weaknesses*

On the other hand, you may not have the ability to listen and question appropriately, or follow instructions and rules. You may not be able to work alone, be at work on time or follow the dress code.

▣▣▣ EVIDENCE ACTIVITY

What makes you tick?

1   Make four copies of the table on the next page.

2   On one copy, rate yourself. Take your time and answer honestly.

3   Get two other people to each complete a copy, giving their opinion on **YOU**.

4   Compare the three copies.

5   Fill out the fourth copy with the average of the scores.

6   Compare the average copy with your original assessment.

7   Comment on the differences — are your scores better or worse? Do you think you have now got areas you should try to improve?

Matching strengths to job roles

Once you understand more about yourself you should investigate companies in the IT sector, and jobs you would like to do. You need to find out enough about them to decide whether or not this is for you. If you are going to find a job that matches your motivation and skills, you need to be very clear about what you want to do, why you want to do it and what skills and knowledge you have.

▣▣▣ EVIDENCE ACTIVITY

Match your skills to jobs in IT

1   Use trade papers, the Internet or other available resources to find at least three job descriptions of the type of job you would like to do. Concentrate on the skills, qualities and qualifications required.

2   List the requirements under the job title.

3   Compare the job requirements with the list you have prepared of your own skills, etc.

4   Do they match?

5   Find job descriptions that do match your own skills.

WHAT MAKES YOU TICK?

Assessment of: _____   By: _____

Read the statements and tick one of the boxes, **5** being the **highest** rating.

	1	2	3	4	5
I take charge when with other people					
I do not like people who do not do their best					
I can deal with difficult people					
I can do anything I set my mind to					
I prefer working with a difficult but highly competent person rather than a friendly, less competent one					
I enjoy accomplishing complex tasks by myself					
I am able to work alone					
I believe I can influence results					
I can analyse complex situations quickly					
I push myself to complete tasks					
I can work long hours if necessary					
I need to be the best at whatever I do					
I do not become frustrated easily					
I thrive on challenges					
I dislike settling into an unchanging routine					
I would rather use my initiative than being told what to do					
I have a higher energy level than most					
I can change my course of action if something is not working					

Add all the figures to make a total: _____

Action plans

If you want to succeed you must set goals. It is helpful if you set out a plan with staged targets. There should also be a timetable attached to these targets – for example, this year I will complete the Level 2 assessment, next year I will undertake the Level 3 assessment.

The aim of an action plan is to achieve your goals. Your plan must include all the steps required to achieve your goals, and can have targets along the way. It may be, say, a five-year action plan, but it helps if the targets are fairly short term. Your plan may be a personal plan, or it may be that it is combined with your personal and professional development plan at work.

The important thing is to decide on your goals, set up the plan and then monitor your progress. The targets will help you to do this. When you reach a target (or if you have failed to reach a target in the time you had specified) you should review your plan. If you do begin to have difficulties with your progress, re-evaluate. If you do not, you may end up not achieving your goals.

▨▨▨ EVIDENCE ACTIVITY

Prepare an action plan

1   Select a job that you think you would like to be doing in five years time — your goal.

2   Set up an action plan so that you will be in a position to do the job at that time. You will need to set up a timetable of the targets you are aiming for.

You should consider the qualifications you will need, how you will get them, and think about how you will pay for them. For example, is there a company that may offer this type of development path, and pay for it?

You will also need to consider the skills that the job requires that you need to acquire or develop.

You should specify when and how you will monitor your progress, and when you will review your plan.

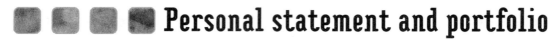

Personal statement and portfolio

Personal statement

A good CV (Curriculum Vitae) demonstrates self-awareness and research. These allow you to target a specific sector, or a specific employer and job. You must understand how your skills and experience can transfer to your career. It is up to you to show your most important attributes and to make them relevant to the job. You must research the job and sector and find out the qualifications, skills and experience an employer wants.

For advertised jobs you may obtain a job description. For other applications you may have to do the work yourself using the company website, job profiles and by talking to people already working in that kind of job.

You should help the reader to focus on the important information that your CV contains. It should be easy to read. The use of bullet points can help keep information concise. Be positive and direct. Put your main selling points on the first page – these may be qualifications but could be particularly relevant work experience or key skills. Be selective – you do not have a lot of space, so only give relevant information.

● ● ● *Details*

Your CV, which you should limit to two pages of A4, should include the following sections:

Personal details	Name, address, date of birth, telephone number, etc. Many people now include a passport-sized photograph with their CV. In some cases, a company may ask you to do so.
Education	Put the most important qualification first – usually the highest and most recent.
Employment	Concentrate on identifying relevant and transferable skills you have gained during work or work experience.
Other skills	Include skills or qualifications such as First Aid or Life Saving.
Interests	If you have limited formal work experience, listing hobbies and interests may be the best way of showing particular skills and qualities. Keep them short, truthful and as relevant as possible to the skills or personality type the job demands.
Referees	Usually include the names of two people who have agreed to provide a reference for you.

TIPS

Here are some tips that will help you:

- *List technical knowledge first*: use technical terms to describe your knowledge and experience. For example, you could list the operating systems and software you have used; or the programming languages you know.
- *Don't sell yourself short*: this is by far the biggest mistake. Treat your CV as an advertisement – sell yourself by highlighting all your strengths.
- *Omit unnecessary details*: leave out any unnecessary information such as your National Insurance number.
- *Review it*: choose someone attentive to details, who can comment on the content and presentation. No matter how many times you read it, mistakes can slip through. Proofread several times. Check spelling, grammar, punctuation and capitalisation.
- *Presentation*: use a font that will be easy to read, photocopy or scan. Print on plain white, quality paper.

• • • On-line CVs

It is now quite common to use on-line CVs or to send CVs by email. On-line CVs usually have an application form format. If you send your CV by email be aware that different browsers can affect formatting – so that a carefully designed and formatted CV may be changed.

▦▦▦ EVIDENCE ACTIVITY

Prepare a curriculum vitae

1   Gather all the information you require to prepare your CV.

2   Produce your CV using suitable software. Include your photograph (for help with using Word, see Unit 9).

Portfolio

• • • Application forms

The purpose of application forms is to standardise the format and content of applicant details so that a company can compare them more quickly. They want to see if there is a match between the skills, qualities and knowledge of applicants and those required for the job.

Companies are under pressure of time to select those they wish to interview from large numbers of applicants. It is easier for them to find reasons to reject, rather than accept applications. One of the reasons employers report for rejecting applicants is spelling and grammatical errors. A recurring comment was that they could tell those who had really taken time in preparing it.

Before you fill in an application form, make a copy of it. You can then prepare a draft on the copy. When you are happy with your draft, complete the original form. It should be legible and neat.

TIPS

When filling in a form it is important that you consider these points:

- Read all the instructions before you fill it in.
- Make sure you understand and follow all the instructions.
- Answer the questions asked – not the questions you want to answer.
- Put qualifications in descending chronological order – your latest first.
- Be accurate. Make sure grades and dates are correct.
- Fit your answers into the space given.
- Make sure it is clear and legible.
- Check the spelling and grammar, and get someone else to check it too.
- Keep a copy – it will be useful at your interview.

GIVE IT A GO | fill in an application form

1 Find an advertisement for a job you would like to do.
2 Get an application form for the job.
3 Following the advice above, complete the application form.
4 Attach the advertisement, and any other materials used to research the position, to the form.

• • • A letter of application

This used to be handwritten, but today it is more usual, and acceptable, to produce a word processed document. It will have either your CV or an application form with it. It is also referred to as a *covering letter*. It should make the employer want to read your CV or application form, and invite you for interview. It provides the opportunity to show your personality and individuality.

It should be targeted at the specific job and should demonstrate the skills you have that are most relevant to it.

TIPS

It is a simple document – just follow these rules:

- Lay it out as a formal business letter. Put your name at the bottom and remember to sign it.
- Send it to a *named* person. If you do not know the correct name, ring the company to find out.
- Keep it concise – a single A4 page with four or five relevant paragraphs:
  - The first paragraph should include: why you are writing; the name of the post you are applying for; where you have seen the advertisement.
  - The two or three central paragraphs should concentrate on highlighting the particular ways you meet the specification of the person the company is looking for, and the relevant skills, qualifications and experience you have.
  - In the final paragraph look forward confidently, such as putting, 'I look forward to meeting you in the near future'.
- If applying to a company where creativity is part of the job such as a web design company, it is all right to make your application a little different. It is important to be original, but not too extreme.

• • • *A letter of acceptance*

This is a letter that you write if, following an interview, you have been offered a job and you wish to accept it. Again, it used to be hand written, but now you can use a word processed document.

TIPS

Keep it simple – follow these rules:

- Lay it out as a formal business letter. Put your name at the bottom and remember to sign it.
- Keep it concise – a single A4 page.
- Send it to the person who is named on the letter offering you the job.
- Thank them for offering the job and accept the offer.
- You may use it to clarify points such as start date if this has not been specified.

GIVE IT A GO | write a covering letter

1 Write a covering letter to use with the application form you completed in the previous activity.
2 Imagine that Mr John White has written to you offering you the job. Write a letter of acceptance.

• • • *Preparation for interviews*

Presentation

There are a number of things that you need to do to prepare yourself for an interview. One of them is deciding on the clothes that you will wear. They should make you look like you will fit in at the company. Dress in a business-like, professional manner.

Males should wear smart business clothing, preferably a suit and a pressed shirt. Avoid flashy ties – prove you are an individualist through your skills and knowledge not your clothing. Do not wear jewellery such as an earring.

Females should also wear smart business clothing. Avoid wearing jewellery and makeup that are showy or distracting. Forget excessively long fingernails and if you wear nail polish, make sure it is a subtle and neat.

Hair should be clean and well-groomed. Shoes should be polished. Avoid heavy, or too much aftershave or perfume. How you dress and your overall appearance will be noticed. Do not rule yourself out because you did not iron your shirt or polish your shoes.

Communication skills

In an interview your abilities will be judged on your communication skills. It is your chance to show someone you are well-prepared, mature and competent. Listen carefully to questions. If you do not understand, ask for an explanation.

An interview is a conversation, not a one-way dialogue. It is an opportunity for the company to get to know you through what you say and how you say it. Be polite, but try to display confidence in yourself. Remember, it is also a chance for you to get to know the company. Prepare a few questions about the company or the job that you would like to have answered.

TIPS

Here are some interview tips that will help you:

- *Do not get too nervous*: Try to relax – think about how the interview will go. Remember the interviewer is just another person; so be professional, but be yourself. Take your time when answering questions.

- *Be well prepared*: Get information on the company. You can never be too prepared for an interview. The company's website should help you.

- *Expect the question 'Tell me a little about yourself?'*: It is impossible to know what an interviewer will ask, but this is one of the most popular questions.

- *Do not smoke or drink alcohol before the interview*: The interviewer will be able to detect both, and may find them offensive.

- *Take the appropriate materials*: CV, references or other items you have asked to bring, and take pens for filling in forms.

- *Get to the interview at least 15 minutes before the arranged time*. If you are not sure of the location, you should check it before the day of the interview.

• • • *Interview questions*

It is important to think about questions you might like to ask at an interview. The questions you ask will depend on the company, the job and also on what you are interested in. Although the canteen facilities and coffee machine may be your priority, there are other things. To help you, here are some examples:

- What would be a typical day in this job?
- What training is available?
- Is there a typical career path for someone in this position?
- How are employees evaluated?
- What would I have to do to be promoted?
- How long would it be before I could get a promotion?

GIVE IT A GO   interview preparation

The questions below are typical of what you might be asked at an interview. You should prepare yourself. Provide written answers to these questions.

- What sort of person are you?
- How does your family describe you?
- What are you good at?
- What are you best at?
- Are there any things you do not like doing?
- What do you find difficult?
- Do you find it difficult to work with some people? Describe them.
- Do you leave things to the last minute or always meet deadlines?
- What gives you a feeling of satisfaction?
- What do you think you can do for us?
- What special skills have you got?
- Why do you want this job?
- Why should we take you on?
- How will you fit in?
- Are you ambitious?
- What would your ideal job include?
- What other kind of work would you like to do?

... *you were called to an interview*

Arrange interviews for your group – this activity may be carried out in smaller groups of four or five. It would be useful if these could be recorded so that you can review your performance. Alternatively, you will have to observe each other – some people may be put off by this.

You should get someone suitable to do the interviewing. They should be given the list of questions above, and they can ask no more than two questions of their own.

You should approach this interview as if it is for a job that you really want – you should treat it seriously, dress appropriately, etc.

As each candidate is being interviewed (or on the replay), make notes on these aspects:

- Did they give good, well-prepared answers?
- Were they dressed appropriately?
- What were their body language and posture like?
- Do you think they had prepared well enough?
- Were they calm?
- Did they listen to the questions?
- What do you think they could improve on?
- Any other comments?

unit 5

Social responsibility at work

In this unit you will learn how you can make a difference in your workplace. It has been designed to help you to understand that you can help to make changes. You will look at your place of work, the environment in which you work, and why it is important to have laws to protect you and your colleagues. This unit could be completed during a period of work experience or work shadowing using simple survey and observation techniques such as questionnaires, interviews, discussion, or observation checklists.

In this unit you will need to learn about:

▷ environmental issues in work

▷ the law and how it affects people in work.

 # Environmental issues at work

Energy conservation and recycling

Many of the items that we use can have an adverse effect on the environment. If you consider paper, for example, think of the number of trees that are cut down each year to satisfy our need for this product. We all need to think about the consumables we are using at work. Perhaps we could spend a little longer checking our work before printing, for example.

Many companies are now trying to become more environmentally friendly, not only in the design and presentation of their products, but also in how they may be disposed of. You can look at a company's policy on environmental issues before you purchase their products.

• • • *Biodegradable materials*

Biodegradable materials are made from biological, renewable raw materials. When living micro-organisms break down organic material into carbon dioxide, water and mineral salts, in the presence of oxygen, it is called *biodegradation*.

The chemical nature of many detergents, plastics, packaging materials, and medical wastes makes them resistant to degradation.

As it is increasingly important, we have to be creative in finding new ways to deal with waste products. Few people see waste as a resource, but it is a challenge to which we must apply ourselves. One of the problems is that recycling may not be cost-effective.

Packaging is usually made from paper, glass, metal, or plastic. Plastic packaging causes the most concern because recycling is not as straightforward as for the others.

Traditionally plastics are made from petroleum-based materials that are produced from non-renewable oil and are not biodegradable. Polymers of biological origin are now being used as raw materials for plastics. These bioplastics are claimed to be more environmentally friendly. We should be trying not only to reduce packaging, but also to use only biodegradable packaging.

• • • *Recycling inkjet and toner cartridges*

In the UK alone it is estimated that more than 30,000,000 empty printer cartridges are dumped into landfill sites every year. Worldwide this figure increases to over 375,000,000. Recycling printer cartridges decreases the amount of waste.

Given the choice most people would rather dispose of their empty cartridges in a way that would both benefit the environment and raise funds for a good cause. There are organisations that collect and recycle old and empty inkjet and toner cartridges. They will pay you for each empty printer cartridge you return, as well as paying the postal costs.

| GIVE IT A GO | environmental policies |

1   Log on to the Internet.
2   Select two companies and investigate their environmental policies. One useful site is the Hewlett Packard site, but there are many others.
3   Do you think they are doing enough about the environment?
4   What else do you think they could do?
5   What else do you think you could do?

Cleaner environment

● ● ● *Air quality*

Air pollution means any harmful gases getting into the air we breathe. It leads to poor air quality. Air pollutants can be released from natural sources, but humans are responsible for much of the pollution. The main sources of air pollution are cars, factories and power stations.

The number of cars in the UK is increasing. Most of the vehicles run on petrol or diesel. All cars made now can run on unleaded petrol. Lead pollution can be particularly harmful to children, and can be damaging to wildlife.

Cars using unleaded petrol emit other pollutants, including carbon monoxide, nitrogen oxides and particulates – all emitted from exhausts. All new cars sold in the UK since 1993 have had to have catalytic converters to reduce these emissions.

We use electricity to cook food, watch television and make our daily lives more comfortable. Electricity is produced in power stations. To do so, they burn coal, oil and gas and release sulphur dioxide and nitrogen oxides. In the UK, 90 per cent of sulphur dioxide pollution comes from power stations and industry.

Ozone is another major pollutant. It is formed when air pollutants react together in sunlight to form smog.

Air pollution causes a number of problems in the environment – it affects our health as we depend on air to live and breathe. Vegetation and wildlife are also affected – sulphur dioxide and nitrogen oxides contribute to acid rain, which affects lakes, trees, and wildlife.

There are many ways to reduce air pollution, for example using buses and trains instead of cars, which can carry far more people in one journey. Walking or cycling are even more beneficial, as they do not create any pollution. They can also benefit health, as regular exercise keeps you fitter.

If you must use a car, avoid using it for very short journeys. If driving to work or the shops try to share journeys with other people.

We can help to prevent pollution by turning off lights and not wasting electricity. This will reduce the demand and less electricity will need to be produced. Less coal, oil and gas will have to be burnt, resulting in less air pollution.

• • • Litter and waste

Litter is a growing problem in our society. We need to change attitudes towards litter and waste. Most people would prefer not to find fast food wrappers in the garden or fly-posting on walls and lamp posts. Nor do we want to see spaces where rubbish has been tipped, and cars have been abandoned. Local authorities are responsible for removing litter.

In March 2001, the Minister for the Environment announced his intention to develop a Voluntary Code of Practice for members of the fast food industry to reduce the levels of fast food litter and waste. This has led to the development of a framework to reduce litter and waste in the local environment, without significant extra cost to the industry. The Voluntary Code of Practice was released for consultation in October 2003. Following the consultation, a series of recommendations was compiled to help to develop the final Code of Practice.

WHAT if

... we continue to ignore recycling or waste?

1 Log on to the Internet and access the website **www.rethinkrubbish.com**.

2 The website gives information on the growing problem of household rubbish in the UK, and some ideas about solving the problem. Look around the website to see the kind of activities on the site.

Health policies in the workplace

• • • Anti-smoking policy

Over the last few years, pressure has been mounting around the world for controls on passive smoking in the workplace, often led by trade unions. Britain's workers say their right to a smoke-free working environment far outweighs the right of people to smoke.

Passive smoking, which means breathing air containing cigarette smoke, is harmful and can cause a range of illnesses. This is why employers, who have a duty to protect their staff from harmful substances, must make sure that non-smokers are not exposed to tobacco smoke in the air.

The three main problems caused by smoking at work are:

• *Harm to non-smokers*: passive smoking can cause problems for asthma and bronchitis sufferers. as it impairs general lung function.

- *Smoking is the largest cause of preventable disease*: associated with many diseases including heart disease.
- *Lost productivity*: a smoker taking five breaks a day for a cigarette does not spend that time at their desk. One study estimated that a single smoker costs his or her employer more than £1,000 a year in lost time. There is also increased risk of absenteeism because of ill health. Non-smokers can feel aggrieved at having to breathe poor quality air and see smokers taking frequent breaks.

Other costs to companies where employees smoke at work include cleaning, decorating and higher insurance premiums because of fire risk.

Research has shown that good air quality can raise productivity. It helps if companies have a scheme for those who want to give up. Studies show that the cost of providing such help can be repaid by associated gains in productivity and attendance.

• • • Anti-alcohol policy

Alcohol can affect work performance through impairment of skills. Alcohol affects efficiency and safety – it increases the likelihood of mistakes and errors of judgement. Constant heavy drinking can lead to a range of problems including dependence. It is associated with poor performance. There may be increased sickness leave and lateness. Absence from work connected with alcohol costs companies millions of pounds each year.

• • • Temperature policy

The law requires that a reasonable temperature should be kept in indoor workplaces during working hours. No maximum or minimum temperature is specified. Heating systems should not allow harmful or offensive fumes to enter the workplace. Keeping a comfortable temperature may include: providing air conditioning; placing workstations away from heat sources; insulation; shading windows; and providing suitable protective clothing.

• • • Humidity policy

Controlling humidity is essential for comfort in all workplaces. Humidity is the amount of moisture in the air. Low levels can make respiratory and skin conditions worsen. There may be a build up of static electricity in dry air, resulting in shocks. If humidifiers are used to moisten the air they must be properly cleaned and maintained.

• • • Ventilation policy

Every enclosed workplace must have effective and suitable ventilation to provide fresh or purified air. The build up of impure air can result in *sick building syndrome* – where occupants suffer respiratory and other illnesses. In many cases, windows provide sufficient ventilation. Other solutions would be to install air inlets and air conditioning systems.

• • • *Lighting policy*

Every workplace should have suitable lighting – wherever possible it should be natural light. Lighting should enable people to work, use facilities and move about safely without experiencing eye-strain.

Exposure to fluorescent lighting is associated with headache, eye-strain, eye irritation, fatigue and increased stress and accidents. Flickering lighting may produce hyperactivity. A shortage of natural light can lead to SAD (Seasonal Affective Disorder).

Good lighting conditions involve:

- maximum natural daylight
- avoiding fluorescent lighting where possible
- maximum control by individual workers of ambient lighting including the provision of desk lights and uplighters
- avoidance of dazzle and glare
- suitable lighting for both indoor and external traffic routes
- suitable positioning of light switches
- immediate repair or replacement of all faulty lights, light fittings and cabling.

If workers could be exposed to danger when artificial lighting fails, there should be sufficient, suitable emergency lighting.

• • • *VDU radiation policy*

Natural background radiation is a fact of life. We are all exposed to it: we breathe small amounts of the radioactive gas *radon*; the ground and buildings are slightly radioactive; our bodies contain natural radioactivity from food and drink; cosmic rays fall on us all the time.

There are two types of radiation: non-ionising electromagnetic radiation (mostly from light and electromagnetic fields such as those generated by overhead powerlines) and naturally occurring ionising radiation.

The Ionising Radiations Regulations 1999 (IRR99) require employers to keep exposure to ionising radiations as low as they reasonably can. Exposures must not exceed specified dose limits. Restrictions of exposure should be achieved first by means of engineering control and design features. Where this is not reasonably practicable, employers should introduce safe systems of work and only rely on the provision of personal protective equipment as a last resort.

VDUs give out both visible light, which allows you to see the screen, and other forms of electromagnetic radiation, which can be harmful above certain levels. The levels of radiation from VDUs are well below the safe levels set out in international recommendations. Your employer does not have a duty to check radiation levels from VDUs.

> ### GIVE IT A GO   company health policies
>
> 1 Select three companies – only one should be in the IT field, one should be a company involved in transport and the third should be a manufacturing company.
> 2 For each company, investigate their policy relating to smoking and alcohol in the workplace – do they have a policy, do they provide any facilities for smokers or help for those who want to quit, and what is their policy regarding alcohol?
> 3 Compare the results from the different companies.

Health and hygiene relating to work

• • • *Personal cleanliness*

Personal hygiene is important not only in the workplace, but also for your general good health. Elementary cleanliness is essential – your hair, skin, teeth, hands and nails should be washed regularly and kept clean. You should have access in the workplace to washing facilities to enable you to, at least, keep your hands clean.

You should wash hands thoroughly before and after food and after visiting the toilet. There should be a method of drying your hands, such as an air machine, or disposable towel. If it is an ordinary towel, it should be changed regularly.

Hygiene problems that may cause problems in the workplace include:

- *Bad breath*: poor oral hygiene and infection of gums results in a bad mouth odour called *halitosis*. Smoking can make this worse. Correct brushing and oral care can get rid of bad breath, but there can be other reasons for bad breath, such as colds, sinuses, throat infections or tonsils.
- *Body odour*: the body perspires to keep the body temperature from rising. Sweat is 99 per cent water, and has a small quantity of urea, salt and other compounds. The body has nearly two million sweat glands. Fresh perspiration, when allowed to evaporate, does not cause body odour. An offensive smell is caused when bacteria start to decompose the sweat. Deodorants or antiperspirants can help.

• • • *Private health insurance*

In the UK we have the National Health Service. However, because of the demands made on it, you may have to wait before you can receive treatment. More people are now taking out private health care. In many cases this is provided by employers.

Depending on the amount of money that you pay, you can expect services such as:

- full in-patient treatment such as operations
- a range of outpatient treatments

- specialist consultations and diagnostic procedures, including pathology, radiology, scans, radiotherapy and chemotherapy
- treatment by osteopaths, chiropractors, physiotherapists, homeopaths and acupuncturists.

More expensive policies also include cover for psychiatric, travel and dental needs, home nursing costs, chiropody, recuperative care and incidental hospital expenses such as telephone calls, newspapers etc.

There are other policies related to health, such as:

Critical illness policies

This type of policy is also known as Serious Illness Insurance. It pays a lump sum if you are diagnosed with one of a number of specified critical illnesses. You can use the money as you choose. It may be used to pay debts such as a mortgage, but most people use it to provide an income if they become too ill to continue working.

Income Replacement policies

This type of policy provides an income if you cannot work because of long-term sickness or injury. You get an income, usually equivalent to 50 to 65 per cent of your normal salary, if you are unable to work for a long time. It is usually paid until you reach retirement age, but will stop if you return to work.

If you are self-employed, the income paid is calculated on the amount of your taxable income, or profits, during the 12-month period prior to your becoming unable to work.

Alternative methods of transport

Rather than using a car people are being encouraged to use alternative methods of transport to go to work, to the shops or for school runs. These include:

● ● ● *Walking*

One scheme to encourage this method of transport is called the **Walking Bus,** which is aimed at children aged between 5 and 11 years, as a safe and healthy way for children to walk to and from school. Each 'bus' has an adult volunteer *driver* at the front and *conductor* at the back. It follows a set route, based on where the children live and assessed by a road safety officer, and picks up children at pre-arranged bus stops.

● ● ● *Cycling*

Cycling is thought of as a healthy option, as it provides exercise and is carried out in the fresh air. Cycling as a means of transport is common in European cities such as Amsterdam – and it reduces the number of cars in the city. In this country traffic lanes have been introduced that are for the use of cyclists. Given the traffic congestion, it can be one of the quickest ways to get around major cities.

• • • *Public transport*

Trains

Given our crowded roads, trains are probably the quickest way of getting from A to B – certainly for medium to long journeys – and are less polluting than cars or aeroplanes. In recent times, however, there has been growing dissatisfaction with our train services. Watchdogs report that they are expensive, and provide poor service in terms of punctuality, and provision. Nevertheless, trains provide a good countrywide service for the majority of people, and, particularly in major cities, thousands of people use trains to get to work every day.

Trams

These are coming back into fashion as a mode of transport. They have been hailed as a new innovation in this country, although many of us can remember tram systems being removed during the 1960s. Many European cities use trams as the means of transport around their cities, and the UK has begun to reintroduce them.

Underground trains

These are usually based in major cities. Because they are below ground they do not cause congestion. In London, where the largest underground system in the country is operated, millions use the system each week. Other cities that use underground systems include Glasgow, Newcastle and Liverpool.

Buses

Buses and coaches accounted for only one per cent of motor vehicle traffic in 2002. However, buses are the most widely-used form of public transport. Over 4.3 billion journeys were made by local bus in the UK in 2001/02, more than twice the number of journeys made by rail. Travel in London accounts for about a third of journeys on local buses. The Government aims to promote bus use in order to reduce traffic congestion and pollution. It has a target to increase bus use in England by ten per cent from 2000 levels by 2010.

> **GIVE IT A GO** getting to work
>
> 1   Decide on a location that you might travel to from your home.
> 2   Investigate how much it would cost to make the journey by rail, on the bus (or coach), in a car, and by cycling, and how long each journey might take.

• • • *New developments in transport*

Congestion charging

Congestion charging has been introduced in London to make sure that those using congested roads pay for it, and to try to make journey times quicker. It has been accompanied by a range of measures to try to make public transport easier, cheaper, faster and more reliable. If you want to drive in central London during the hours of operation it now costs £5 per day. It was introduced because:

- London has the worst traffic congestion in the UK and is among the worst in Europe
- drivers in central London spend 50 per cent of their time in queues
- every weekday, the equivalent of 25 motorway lanes of traffic tries to enter central London
- it has been estimated that London loses between £2–4 million every week in terms of lost time caused by congestion.

Other cities in Europe and the UK are considering schemes to reduce congestion. So far, no other city has implemented such a scheme.

Alternative fuels

Alternative fuels are being used in place of petroleum-based fuels. Their use helps to reduce dependence on imported petroleum. They include bio-diesel, electricity, ethanol, hydrogen, methanol, natural gas, propane, p-series, and solar energy.

Electric vehicles have lower fuel and maintenance costs, but have high initial costs. The UK has one of the largest electric vehicle fleets in the world – but most are milk floats. There are not many private vehicles, and not many models widely available – Peugeot makes an electric car, but it is currently sold only to businesses not to private individuals; Ford has an electric car but it cannot be bought outright, only leased for 36 months.

Liquefied petroleum gas is the generic term for commercial propane and butane. When used as a fuel, it produces less harmful emissions than either petrol or diesel. Burning LPG reduces carbon dioxide emissions by 11–13 per cent. Petrol engine vehicles can have a gas system installed. Conversions add another fuel system to the vehicle, whilst retaining the original, creating a dual fuel vehicle.

▢▢▢▢ EVIDENCE ACTIVITY

Environmental factors

1 Select a job you would like to do.

2 Explain the environmental factors that would be important to you if you were to do that job.

 # The law

Laws are also called Acts of Parliament. The House of Commons and the House of Lords usually debate proposals for new laws. At this stage they are called Bills. When both Houses agree to the proposals, the Bill is ready to become an Act of Parliament, but it is only described as such when it has received Royal Assent from the queen.

Many Acts include powers that allow government ministers to draw up the detailed rules needed to make them work. This is known as secondary or delegated legislation: Parliament has the opportunity to refuse secondary legislation or, in some cases, approve it before it takes effect.

How the law helps you at work

There are laws to protect workers and employers. Workplace safety and health laws establish regulations designed to eliminate personal injuries or illness in the workplace. They also provide regulations for safety and health standards to protect employers and employees.

Inspectors inspect premises to ensure that regulations are being followed. They also examine conditions if complaints are made, and decide on any actions that may be required. If an employer is violating regulations they have to take action. Fines can be imposed depending on the type of violation and length of non-compliance.

There are laws that cover the hours you work, the number and duration of breaks, the temperature in which you can be expected to work, and environmental factors such as air quality and lighting.

Health and Safety at Work etc Act 1974

This Act sets out the main principles of health and safety law:

- Employers have to look after the health, safety and welfare of all their employees
- Employees and the self-employed have to look after their own health and safety
- Everyone has to take care of the health and safety of others, for example, members of the public who may be affected by their work.

Employers fulfil the terms of the Act through company policies such as those outlined on pages 75–80. The Act also specifically covers IT environments. (See Unit 3, page 54, for more details.)

Secondary legislation associated with the Act includes:

- *The Management of Health and Safety at Work Regulations 1992*: These place duties on companies and individuals to ensure that adequate provisions are made for health and safety at work.
- *The Workplace (Health, Safety and Welfare) Regulations 1992*: These regulations are specifically aimed at protecting the health and safety of everyone in the workplace, and ensuring that adequate welfare facilities are provided.

A health and safety warning on the back of a CPU

Other laws affecting you at work

There is a large amount of legislation covering the workplace. Here are the key Acts, in chronological order:

• • • *Equal Pay Act 1970*

This Act applies to women and men of any age, including children in England, Wales and Scotland. It gives an individual a right to the same contractual pay and benefits as a person of the opposite sex in the same employment, where the man and the woman are doing: the same job; work rated as equivalent under an analytical job evaluation study; or work that is proved to be of equal value.

Employers are not required to provide the same pay and benefits if they can prove that the difference is not related to sex.

• • • *Sex Discrimination Act 1975*

This Act applies to women and men of any age, including children in England, Wales and Scotland. It prohibits sex discrimination against individuals in the areas of: employment; education; the provision of goods, facilities and services; the disposal or management of premises.

It prohibits discrimination in employment against married people, but it is not unlawful to discriminate against someone because they are not married. Employees have rights under this Act whatever their length of employment and whatever hours they work.

In general, positive discrimination to favour one sex is not lawful. There are limited exceptions allowing discrimination in training, or encouragement to apply for particular work in which members of the relevant sex are under-represented. These lawful exceptions are often referred to as positive action.

• • • *Race Relations Act 1976*

This Act prohibits discrimination on racial grounds in the areas of: employment; education; and the provision of goods, facilities and services and premises. Following changes made by the Race Relations (Amendment) Act 2000, there is also now a positive duty on public authorities to eliminate unlawful discrimination and promote equality of opportunity.

• • • *Computer Misuse Act 1990*

This Act makes it illegal to gain unauthorised access to or make unauthorised modification of computer material. (See Unit 3, page 55, for more details.)

• • • *Disability Discrimination Act 1995*

This Act deals with discrimination against disabled people in the areas of: employment; the provision of goods, facilities and services and premises; and education and public transport.

• • • *Pensions Act 1995*

This Act requires occupational pension schemes to observe the principle of equal treatment between men and women.

• • • *Employment Rights Act 1996*

This Act includes the following rights:

- The right not to be unfairly dismissed. A dismissal is automatically unfair if it is related to pregnancy, childbirth, maternity leave, parental leave, or time off for dependants.
- The right to maternity leave.
- The right to paid time off for ante-natal care.
- The right to unpaid time off to care for, or to arrange care for, dependants where the dependant is ill, injured, assaulted, gives birth or dies; if arrangements for the care of a dependant break down; or if there is an unexpected incident involving a child at school.
- The right to be offered suitable alternative work on similar terms and conditions if a health and safety requirement prohibits a woman from doing her usual job because she is pregnant, has recently given birth or is breastfeeding.
- The right to be suspended on full pay if a woman is unable to do her usual job on maternity grounds as described above and no suitable alternative work is available.
- The right to a statement of employment particulars.
- The right to an itemised pay statement.
- The right not to suffer unauthorised deductions from wages.
- The right to a minimum period of notice on termination of employment.
- The right to a redundancy payment.
- The right to a written statement of reasons for dismissal.

• • • *Human Rights Act 1998*

This Act incorporates rights under the European Convention of Human Rights into domestic UK law. People can bring claims against public authorities for breaches of Convention rights. UK courts and tribunals are required to interpret domestic law, as far as possible, in accordance with Convention rights. Convention rights include a right not to be discriminated against on non-exhaustive grounds, which include that of sex.

• • • *National Minimum Wage Act 1998*

This Act provides that workers shall not be paid less than a designated minimum rate per hour. (See Unit 2, Page 16, for more details).

• • • *Employment Relations Act 1999*

This act includes a right to be accompanied at disciplinary or grievance hearings by a trade union official or another of the employer's workers.

• • • *Data Protection Act 1998*

First passed in the UK in 1984, this Act was updated in 1998 and the new regulations came into force on 1 March 2000. It sets out rules for use of personal information not only on computers, but also on some paper records. It allows individuals the right to know what information is held about them. (See Unit 3, page 54, for more details).

• • • *Employment Act 2002 (Flexible working regulations)*

This Act makes changes to maternity, paternity and adoption rights in the Employment Rights Act 1996. From April 2003, there has been a new right for employees to request flexible working.

• • • *Secondary legislation*

Just as there is a large amount of legislation, there is also the associated secondary legislation. Remember, these are the rules that make the Acts work in practice, and include:

Occupational Pension Schemes (Equal Treatment) Regulations 1995
These regulations set out how claims may be made to enforce rights to equal treatment in occupational pension schemes.

Working Time Regulations 1998
These regulations contain provisions regulating working time including:

- a limit of an average of 48 hours work per week (with exceptions)
- daily and weekly rest entitlements and rest breaks
- a right to 4 weeks' paid annual leave and to be paid for accrued but untaken leave on termination of employment
- special provisions relating to night work.

Management of Health and Safety at Work Regulations 1999
These regulations require employers to carry out risk assessments. There are specific obligations on employers to assess risk where there are women of childbearing age at work. Employers may have to alter working conditions or hours of work, offer suitable alternative work or suspend an expectant or new mother on full pay if necessary to avoid risk to the mother or her baby.

Maternity and Parental Leave etc. Regulations 1999
These regulations contain the detail of the rights to maternity and parental leave contained in the Employment Rights Act 1996. They describe the circumstances in which a dismissal will be automatically unfair under the Employment Rights Act 1996, if the dismissal is for a reason related to pregnancy, childbirth, maternity leave, parental leave, or time off for dependants.

National Minimum Wage Regulations 1999
These regulations contain the rules on who qualifies for the national minimum wage and what counts as working time and remuneration for these purposes.

Part-time Workers Regulations 2000

These regulations give part-time workers the right not to be treated less favourably than comparable full-time workers unless the difference in treatment is objectively justifiable. They do not give a right to work part-time.

The Employment Equality (Religion or Belief) Regulations 2003

These regulations prohibit discrimination in employment on the grounds of religion or belief.

The Employment Equality (Sexual Orientation) Regulations 2003

These regulations prohibit discrimination in employment on the grounds of sexual orientation.

▣▣▣ EVIDENCE ACTIVITIES

Laws in the IT industry

1   Select a job in the IT industry.

2   Describe the laws that are most important to that job in terms of:
  - gender
  - race
  - religion
  - disability
  - sex
  - age.

3   Explain why you think these laws exist.

4   Do you think they will affect you at work? Why?

The importance of work-related laws

As you have seen there is a great deal of legislation regarding employment.

1   Draw up a list of work–related laws. Make two copies.

2   On one copy, grade the items on the list.
  1 = most important.
  2 = important.
  3 = less important.

3   Start with the items graded 1, and explain why you have graded the items as most important.

4   Go on to the items graded 3 and explain why you think the items are less important.

unit 6

Financial management

This unit has been designed to help you to understand how to manage your money. You will see how money is earned. You will think about how you spend your money; you will learn how to balance the money you earn and the money you spend. To demonstrate these skills you will use spreadsheet software.

You will discuss how much you can expect to earn with your current skills, experience and qualifications. You will look at the services that financial institutions, such as banks and building societies, provide.

You will carry out a survey on how your group spends money and prepare a presentation showing the connection between how much money people have and their attitude to budgeting.

In this unit you will learn a method of managing your money.

In this unit you will need to learn about:

▷ sources of income

▷ managing personal finance

▷ how to produce a personal budget using a spreadsheet.

 # Sources of income

At work

• • • *Types of employment*

Most people work to earn money. How that money is paid to them depends on their employment status. The majority of people work for someone else. If the employer provides the work, controls when and how it is done, supplies the tools or other equipment and pays tax and NI on the worker's behalf, then the worker is an *employee*.

Others decide whether or not to accept work and how to carry it out. They make their own payments of tax and NI. They are free to do the same type of work for more than one employer at the same time – the person is *self-employed*. If you use your skills to work for someone else, but you are not an employee of that company you are referred to as a *freelance worker* or a *contractor*.

• • • *Payment*

Gross income is the amount of money that you earn before any statutory deductions are made. Net income is the amount of money that you actually receive.

Basic pay is the amount of money you are paid for the hours you have agreed to work. Other payments may be added to your basic pay, such as *overtime* pay. This is paid when you work more than the agreed hours. It is usually paid at a higher level than basic pay. It may be twice or three times the amount of basic pay. The overtime rate may vary if you work on a Saturday or Sunday or Bank Holidays (if working on those days was not originally part of your contract). Bonuses may be paid if, for example, sales targets are achieved. The amount will normally be based on your basic pay. It is almost always a discretionary payment – the employer does not have to pay it.

Deductions

• • • *Income tax*

This is a *statutory* contribution – by law it must be paid. If you are self-employed you are responsible for making tax payments yourself – usually once a year.

If you are employed your tax payments are PAYE (Pay As You Earn). They are made weekly or monthly (depending on how you are paid). It is taken from your salary by your employer who is then responsible for making the payment to the Inland Revenue.

The rate of tax that you have to pay will depend not only on how much you earn but also on the allowances you are permitted. These allowances also vary.

• • • *National insurance*

This is also a statutory contribution. It is deducted from your salary by your employer who is then responsible for making the payment.

• • • *Pensions*

This contribution is not a compulsory deduction from your salary. You may join a pension scheme in your company, and if so the agreed amount will be taken from your salary.

• • • *Union subscriptions*

You can arrange for your employer to pay your union subscriptions directly from your salary. This is not a compulsory deduction.

• • • *Charitable donations*

These can be made through your salary. Your employer can pay a specified amount to the charity you name. The donation is removed before tax is paid and so it costs you less to make it. This is a voluntary contribution.

Benefits

The Department for Work and Pensions (DWP) is responsible for providing benefits and services. They provide a *Benefits and Services A–Z* that gives information about them on their website.

In April 2003 the Government began paying benefits directly into accounts. This method of payment is called *Direct Payment*. By 2005 anyone receiving benefits and state pensions will do so directly into an account of their choice.

Government provides benefits for both the unemployed and those in work, including:

• • • *Benefits for people of working age*

There is a range of benefits and services. By 2006, a new service, Jobcentre Plus, will deliver them. Until then Jobcentres and Social Security offices are responsible. The Inland Revenue deals with tax credits. Some of the benefits are:

Looking for work	Starting or returning to work	In work
Starting your own business	Managing on a low income	Voluntary work
Long-term ill or disabled	Sick and unable to work	In hospital
Early retirement	Visiting or living abroad	Illness/accidents caused by work

• • • *Working family tax credits*

There are two tax credits, Child Tax Credit and Working Tax Credit.

Child Tax Credit is for people who are responsible for at least one child. If you are a lone parent you will receive the payment.

Working Tax Credit is for people who are employed or self-employed who usually do at least 16 hours paid work a week, for at least four weeks. They must be aged 16 or over and responsible for at least one child, or aged 16 or over and disabled, or aged 25 or over and usually work at least 30 hours a week.

The amount of tax credits you receive will depend on your annual income. To be eligible for tax credits, you and/or your partner must be aged 16 or over and usually live in the UK.

• • • *Housing benefit*

Housing benefit, sometimes called rent rebate or rent allowance is paid by local councils. It helps towards your rent. You can claim this benefit if you are on a low income and paying rent. There are special rules if you are single and under 25. You cannot get this benefit if you live in the house of a close relative, or you are a full-time student, unless you are disabled or have children. To work out the benefit, the council will look at:

- income – including earnings, benefits, tax credits and occupational pensions
- savings – your own and your partner's
- circumstances – such as age, the ages and size of your family, whether you or any of your family are disabled, and whether anyone who lives with you could help with the rent.

The council decides if the rent is reasonable, if your home is a reasonable size for you and if the rent is reasonable for the area.

• • • *Council Tax Benefit*

You can claim this benefit if you are on a low income and paying council tax. It is paid by local councils to help towards your council tax. You do not have to be getting any other benefits. You can get it if you already get a discount on your council tax, for example if you live alone. There are special rules for students. To work out the benefit, the council will look at the same things as they do for Housing benefit.

• • • *Other sources of income*

These include:

Interest
This is the money you receive for saving or investing through stocks or shares.

Inheritances
You may receive an inheritance – money from members of your family or friends, usually on their death. You have to pay tax on money that is inherited.

Borrowed money
This is money that you take as a loan from a financial institution, members of your family, or friends. It has to be repaid and you will pay interest on a loan from a

financial institution. You may not pay interest if you borrow money from family or friends. **Note** – in this case, *interest* is the additional money that you will have to pay for borrowing the money. For example, if you borrow £1,000 and the interest rate is 10 per cent, then you will have to pay back £1,100 – the additional £100 being 10 per cent of the original £1,000.

Benefits if you are out of work

Many of the benefits above are also available to you if you are out of work, but your main benefit will be Job Seekers Allowance (JSA). This provides money for people to live on while they are looking for work. There are two types of allowance:

- *Contributory*: This replaces Unemployment Benefit. This is based on your National Insurance contributions from previous jobs.
- *Means tested*: This replaces Income Support for most of those who used to claim it. This supplements the income of those who have a part-time or temporary low-paid income, and are looking for more work.

You claim this allowance at the Jobcentre. You have to fill in two forms: Helping You Back To Work and Jobseeker's Agreement. To claim this allowance you must:

- be available for, capable of, and actively seeking work
- have entered into a Jobseeker's Agreement
- not be in full time education
- be 18 and in Great Britain.

▪▪▪ EVIDENCE ACTIVITIES

Sources of income

1 Explain these terms:
   - contractor
   - gross and net pay
   - tax
   - national insurance.

2 What other income might you be entitled to if you are on a low wage with no savings?

3 You are 19-years-old, not working or studying, unmarried and living with your parents. What benefits are you entitled to?

Produce a report

1 Explain all the items that make up your income.

2 Produce a word-processed report showing the different sources of income available to people if they are, or are not, working.

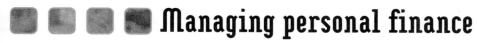 # Managing personal finance

Attitudes to work and money

Managing your personal finances will depend to a great extent on your attitudes to work and money. How you manage your money will also depend on how you have seen others do it (probably your family and friends). Do they spend all their money? What do they spend it on? Do they save?

• • • *Expectations*

Your attitude to money will also depend on your expectations. Do you want to own your own home and car? Do you want to take holidays? Remember, these things cost money. If you want them you will have to plan how to get them. You will probably have to save for them. You need to have a plan for how you deal with, and manage your money.

• • • *Spending and saving*

Spending habits have changed in the recent past. The average household in the UK now has debt of around £8,000, not including mortgages. People are less likely to wait until they can afford an item. The use of credit cards to purchase goods and services has grown dramatically.

Your lifestyle will depend on how much money you earn, but it is also determined by how you manage your money. Be clear about where your money is going. Look at your finances, and work out all your income and spending. Be realistic about what you can afford. Work out how much you can spend and stick to it. Try to save something every month, especially for things like holidays and Christmas.

Use standing orders and direct debits to meet regular outgoings such as rent, mortgage, utility bills and council tax. Some companies offer discounts if you pay by direct debit, so you can save money too. Set up a standing order to a savings account. You will be surprised how quickly you will forget you are saving. Set up the payments to go out a few days after your wages have been paid in.

• • • *Borrowing*

Do your research before borrowing – see what is on offer and get advice. Never borrow money on the spur of the moment. If you are taking out new credit, think carefully about how you would make the repayments if interest rates went up, or if you found yourself out of work. This is especially important in the case of mortgages and secured loans where your home is at risk. If you have a credit card, pay as much as you can off the balance every month. If you can pay for goods outright, do not take out credit unless it meets your overall budgeting plans.

Remember that offers and good ideas can have hidden costs – cheaper monthly payments usually mean that you pay back more in total to the company.

▦▦▦ EVIDENCE ACTIVITY

Thinking about personal finances

1   Copy down the list below into a table. (You may like to do this exercise using a spreadsheet — see Unit 9 for instructions.) Enter the details of how much you spend each month. Add any other items on which you spend money.

Mortgage or rent	Buildings insurance
Contents insurance	Life assurance
Pension	Loan repayments
Gas	Electricity
Council tax	Savings and investments
Telephone	Water rates
Food	Card payments (credit, store)
Car (tax, insurance, petrol) and/or travel	Entertainment (going out, holidays, clothes, etc).

2   When this is done, keep a copy in your evidence folder. You will be using it later.

GIVE IT A GO   attitudes to personal finance

1   Split your class into smaller groups of four or five people.

2   Within your group, carry out a survey on:
   - the amount of money that people have to spend
   - the amount of money that people save
   - why members of your group save.

3   Report back to the other groups in your class with your group findings.

4   From these results, do you see any connection between how much money people have and their attitude to budgeting? For example:
   - Do the people with more money **spend** more than those with less money?
   - Do the people with more money **save** more?
   - Do the people with less money **use credit facilities** more?
   - Do the people with more money **monitor their finances** more carefully?

Using banks, building societies and post offices

At one time financial institutions such as banks, building societies and insurance companies all provided different services. Now the boundaries have become blurred. Most of these financial institutions offer similar services.

There is intense competition for your business. You often see incentives such as *transfer* and *cash back* offers. Many institutions have merged to enable them to compete more successfully. They all offer advice on finances, financial planning, and provide a breakdown of your personal finances – details of the money you have spent, the money paid into your account, etc.

GIVE IT A GO contact financial institutions

It would be useful to approach the banks and building societies in your area and invite representatives to come and present to your group. They can provide information and leaflets to introduce you to their services. If this is not possible, you can get the information from the branches, or from their websites.

The *personal* services you can expect from a bank or building society include:

● ● ● *Current accounts*

You get an account number, a debit card and a cheque book. You will be permitted an overdraft. Some banks check your account each month, and if there are excess funds they are transferred into a savings account. You can pay standing orders and direct debits from your account.

Direct debiting

This is an easy way of paying bills. The money is taken from your account monthly, quarterly or annually by the company who provides the goods or service. You must agree for a company to take a specified amount, on a specified day of the month. For example, you may pay £25 on the second day of each month to your electricity supplier. You can now arrange direct debits over the phone, interactive TV or Internet instead of completing paper instructions. Standing orders are similar but you give the instructions to your bank rather than the company requesting payment from your bank as with a direct debit.

Cash machines

You can access cash machines, paying-in and statement machines with your debit card and your PIN (Personal Identification Number). They allow you to withdraw cash, check and print your balance, print a statement, transfer money between your accounts, change your PIN and order postal statements.

Credit and interest

The bank will expect you to keep your account in *credit*. This means that you do not take more money out of the account than you put in. While your account is in credit, it will earn *interest*. If, on the other hand, you allow your account to go into *debit* (you take out more money than you put in), the bank will charge you an *overdraft* fee – an amount of interest on the money you have, in effect, borrowed from them. The *interest rate* on overdrafts varies.

• • • *Basic Bank Accounts*

This type of account is easy to understand and manage. It is convenient and you have access to your money through cash machines. You do not get an overdraft facility, cheque book, debit or credit cards.

This means that you do not get interest charges or unwanted debt. To open a Basic Bank Account, you must be 18 or over. You get a self-service card; you can use standing orders and direct debits and you receive statements.

Since April 2003 it has been possible to use a Basic Bank Account card to withdraw cash at post offices. You can withdraw up to £200 a day. An exact amount including pence can also be withdrawn at the counter. You need both your card and your PIN to use these facilities.

• • • *Savings accounts*

You may want to save the same amount every month, save when you have some extra cash, or both. There are accounts that allow you to access your money immediately, higher-interest accounts for money you do not need right away, and, for larger amounts, money market accounts and deposit bonds.

With an instant access savings account you get access to your money when you need it, but still get interest. The interest rate may build as your *balance* (the amount you have in your account) grows. Withdrawals can be made at any time and you have the choice of whether interest is paid annually or monthly. High interest savings pay higher interest, but withdrawals are only free if notice is given – such as 60 or 90 days.

Most banks provide free advice on a range of tax-free investments. They inform you about the options available, their benefits and drawbacks, and how suitable they are for you. Options include ISAs. Individual Savings Accounts consist of up to three parts – cash, insurance, and stocks and shares. Each part has a limit. They are tax-free. Currently the total amount you can invest in all three parts is £7,000. You must be over 18 and a UK resident to take out an ISA. However, if you are aged 16 or 17, work, and pay tax, you can invest up to £3,000 in the cash part.

• • • *Loans*

You can obtain loans from very many companies for almost any purpose. You have to show that you will be able to repay the loan. The company providing the loan will often require *security* (an alternative source of payment if you unable to pay the loan back), such as your home. If you need a loan you may approach:

• *A bank or building society, or other financial institutions*: Every day on our TVs and in our mail we are bombarded by companies offering loans. They will lend you money but they will charge interest and may require security.

- *Your family*: They do not normally charge interest. The loan would probably be for a smaller amount and for a shorter time. The family member may accept weekly or monthly payments back.
- *Loan sharks*: These should be avoided at all costs. They charge exorbitant amounts of interest and are known for harsh tactics if you default (fail to meet deadlines) on the payments.

The table below shows an example of the amount of money you would repay each month if you borrowed the amount shown in the first column. It is sensible to take out insurance in case your circumstances change and you are not able to make the repayments.

Loan amount	APR %	12 months		36 months	
		Monthly repayments **with** insurance	Monthly repayments **without** insurance	Monthly repayments **with** insurance	Monthly repayments **without** insurance
£1,000	14.9	£96.06	£89.76	£38.13	£34.18
£4,000	12.5	£379.99	£355.10	£147.86	£132.55
£5,000	08.9	£466.87	£436.29	£176.19	£157.95
£10,000	07.9	£928.99	£868.13	£347.69	£311.69
£15,000	07.9	£1,393.47	£1,302.19	£521.54	£467.54

If you took the loan for 12 months, the amount you would repay is shown in columns 3 and 4 – column 3 with insurance, column 4 without insurance. If you took the loan for 36 months, the amount you would repay is shown in columns 5 and 6 – column 5 with insurance, column 6 without insurance.

The interest rate (APR = Annual Percentage Rate of interest) depends on the loan amount, and in this example is the same for the whole period of the loan. For example, if you borrowed £5,000 over 36 months (without insurance), you would pay total interest of £686.20, giving a total amount of £5,686.20.

GIVE IT A GO borrowing money

1 Find five companies that offer loans.

2 What does each of the companies offer – interest rate, no of years to repay, etc.

3 Complete the figures in this table to compare different companies. The loan should be for £10,000 over five years. Enter the company name in the first column.

	Interest rate %	Monthly repayments **with** insurance	Monthly repayments **without** insurance	Total amount to repay

4 Which deal do you think is the best for you?

5 What did you take into consideration?

• • • Credit cards

A credit card is a method of paying for goods and services. It avoids you having to carry cash. You can use your card as payment or to withdraw an agreed amount of money per day from cash machines. You can have additional cards for your spouse or partner. There is a pre-set credit limit depending on your circumstances.

It is a source of credit – you can purchase items that you cannot afford and then pay back the credit card company over a period of time. The credit card company sends you a statement at the end of each month showing your purchases and payments in the previous month. It will also indicate a minimum amount for you to pay them.

Many people use a credit card just as an alternative to cash. They pay the credit card bill in full at the end of each month. If you do not do this, then the credit card company will charge you interest on the amount of money that is outstanding. The interest rate varies, as do the conditions.

GIVE IT A GO | choosing a credit card

1 Find five companies that offer credit cards.
2 What does each of the companies offer, regarding interest rate, transfer offers, etc?
3 Draw up a table, showing the results.
4 Which do you think is the best card?
5 What did you take into consideration?

Methods of banking

Internet banking

E-banking facilities provide 24-hour on-line access to your accounts. It is now far safer to bank on-line. Companies providing these services use firewalls, secure gateways and monitoring devices to deter hackers. If you submit or download sensitive information, it is encrypted to prevent unauthorised access. They provide you with facilities to: check balances and view transactions; view, amend, create and cancel standing orders; view and cancel direct debits; pay bills and make payments; transfer money between your accounts; and change your address and personal details.

Telephone banking

This allows 24-hour automated banking services, which include: checking your balance; transferring money between your accounts; and hearing details of your latest transactions. During extended business hours you can also speak to staff to pay bills, or make payments.

Text phone banking

With this you can use your text phone to check balances; transfer money between your accounts; pay bills; hear details of your latest transactions and make payments.

TV banking

If you have digital services on your TV you can: view your balances and transactions; move money between bank accounts held in your own name; pay bills and make payments; view, set up, amend and cancel standing orders; view and cancel direct debits; and stop cheques.

• • • *The post office*

You probably know that you can send and receive mail in this country and overseas, and that you can pick up benefits from the post office. You may be surprised to discover the range of other services that are now provided. Many of these are available on-line and over the telephone as well. You can get licenses, a range of service for phones, as well as:

- *Travel services*: This includes travel insurance, foreign currency (commission-free), passport applications services, passport-sized photographs, car hire, and medical care in the EU with an E111 form. You can also carry out international money transfers.
- *Pensions and benefits services*: This includes information on when, how and what to claim, through advice as well as a range of leaflets. Pensions and benefits payments can also be collected, or direct debit payments set up from here. You can get help with a range of health-related services.
- *Personal loans service*: These are offered from £1,000 to £25,000. You can apply on-line or on the phone. Applicants must be 21 or over and a UK resident. You can take out payment protection insurance so that your monthly instalments would be paid in case of accident, sickness, major illness, unemployment or death.
- *Personal banking services*: It is possible to get both a current account and a basic bank account with the post office. It also offers a post office card account – this can only be used to receive benefits, State pensions and new tax credit payments. No other payments, such as wages, can be paid into it. It is a simple account – you cannot get overdrawn or incur charges. You can take cash out, free of charge, at any branch using a plastic card and PIN. You can also use your card and PIN to request a balance enquiry at any branch.
- *Postal orders service*: This is an inexpensive method of sending money. British postal orders can be cashed in 47 countries worldwide. Many countries also sell them.
- *Bill-paying service*: You can pay a range of bills including telephone, cable TV, gas, electricity, water, and TV licence. There are budgeting facilities such as savings stamps or payment cards. You can recharge many electricity keys or gas cards and buy pre-payment tokens for gas and electricity. Bills Online is a free service to view, manage and pay multiple bills on-line.

■■■ EVIDENCE ACTIVITY

Planning an investment

Imagine you have £5,000 to invest. Select a suitable savings account for the money.

You should plan how you will carry out the investigation:
- How many different banks or building societies will you include?
- How many accounts will you include?

1 Gather the information you need — go to the banks or use the Internet.

2 Summarise your findings (some of the data could be presented as graphs):
- Who provides the best result?
- Which is the safest account?

3 Produce a report outlining your findings, including a comparison table.

Running a bank or building society account

● ● ● *Using a cheque book*

If you have a current account you will be provided with a cheque book. Until quite recently, the cheque was probably the most common way of paying for goods and services. People now use credit and debit cards as well.

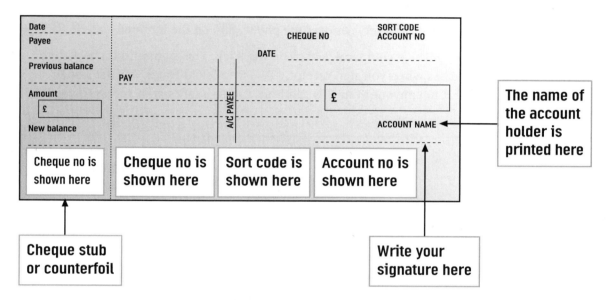

Your cheque book usually contains 30 cheques. Each has information about the bank and your account. Each bank has a code to identify not only the bank, such as NatWest or HSBC, but also which branch of that bank it is. This is called the bank or sort code. Each cheque will have the cheque number, the account number and the name of the account holder printed on it.

To complete a valid cheque you must fill in:

- the date – write this next to the word DATE
- the *exact* name of the person or account you are paying the amount to (the payee) write it next to the word PAY
- the amount you are paying – in words **and** figures. Write the figures in the box next to the £ sign, and the words after the payee name
- your signature – write your signature on the line below the account name.

There is also a cheque stub (*counterfoil*) for you to keep your own record of the transaction on the cheque. You should do this for every cheque to monitor your spending.

● ● ● *Debit cards*

This card is usually issued when you open a current account. Cheques are rarely accepted for payment unless you have a debit card. Your bank guarantees payment by cheque if debit card details are included. This guarantee is only to the limit shown on the card. Unlike a credit card the money you are spending has to be in your account.

You can use your debit card to withdraw money from your account at cash machines. To gain access to your account you will be issued with a PIN. Outside branch hours, banks with ATMs (Automatic Teller Machines) allow access to them by use of your debit card. You can use them to get statements; to check the balance of your account; and to pay for goods and services over the phone, and on the Internet.

As soon as you receive your card, sign it on the back. This signature is checked to ensure it matches when you sign receipts. This is to avoid fraud. For the same reason, NEVER tell anyone your PIN. Without it they cannot gain access to your account.

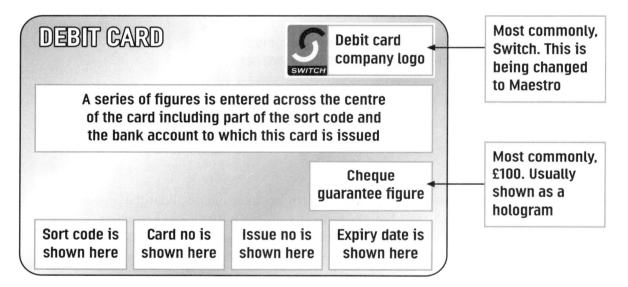

DEBIT CARD

Debit card company logo

Most commonly, Switch. This is being changed to Maestro

A series of figures is entered across the centre of the card including part of the sort code and the bank account to which this card is issued

Cheque guarantee figure

Most commonly, £100. Usually shown as a hologram

| Sort code is shown here | Card no is shown here | Issue no is shown here | Expiry date is shown here |

Personal finance records

It is important to keep records of how you are spending your money. The first thing you should do is check your income – make sure you are being paid the correct amount. Check the deductions – make sure you are on the correct tax rate and that you are receiving the correct allowances, that you have been paid for all the hours you have worked on the appropriate rate, and that any allowances (such as clothing allowances) have been included. All these details should be clear from your wage slips. If you are self-employed it will depend on how carefully you have kept your records as you went along.

You must also check the records of your spending from your:

- *Bank statements*: make sure that the correct amounts have been recorded for money coming into your account and going out including regular payments such as direct debits and standing orders.

- *Credit, debit and store card statements*: to make sure that the correct amounts have been paid. So that you do not have to pay additional interest, pay the bills before the due date.
- *Internet account statements*: home shopping has grown – you can now buy products and services from supermarkets, department stores, holiday companies and the many small businesses that trade on the Internet. You usually pay by debit or credit card. Check that the entries on your statements are correct.

◼◼◻ EVIDENCE ACTIVITY

Managing your personal finances
Produce a word-processed report outlining:

▢ the different places you can put your money

▢ methods of keeping your money safe

▢ how you can monitor your money.

Why do you think it is important to manage your personal finances?

◼ ◼ ◼ ◼ Produce a personal budget

Personal budgeting

To plan the best use of the money you have you must know how much you have. Work out how much you earn, and how much you need to meet your commitments. Make lists of both and then calculate the amount of money you have left. This is called budgeting.

First, write down the money you receive – your income. This includes your salary or wages, any interest on your savings, tips, any benefits you receive, and any bonuses.

Next, write down all the money that you have to spend – your expenditure. This includes regular outgoings including rent, household bills such as gas and electricity bills, council tax, water rates, TV licence, food and cleaning items. You should also include any costs for travelling to work, home insurance, and other outgoings that you need to meet such as leisure activities and holidays.

If you want to buy that new car or take that tropical holiday you will have to plan your income and expenditure over time to meet that goal. A simple method of doing this is to enter the details into a spreadsheet. If you need help on how to use a spreadsheet, see Unit 9, pages 155–159.

GIVE IT A GO — how to create a personal budget

1 Open a spreadsheet program.

2 The example you are going to use shows you how to work out how much money you have remaining each month in a three-month period.

3 Copy Figure 6.1 (including the formulae) into your spreadsheet. Make sure you enter the contents in the cells exactly as shown.

	A	B	C	D	E
1	PERSONAL BUDGET				
2		JAN	FEB	MAR	TOTAL
3	INCOME				
4	Wages	750	750	750	=SUM(B4:D4)
5	Tips	52.35	52.75	45.55	=SUM(B5:D5)
6	Bonuses	25.5	25	32.5	=SUM(B6:D6)
7	Income Total	=SUM(B4:B6)	=SUM(C4:C6)	=SUM(D4:D6)	=SUM(B7:D7)
8					
9	EXPENDITURE				
10	Rent	350	350	350	=SUM(B10:D10)
11	Council Tax	15	15	15	=SUM(B11:D11)
12	Gas and Electricity	15	10	10	=SUM(B12:D12)
13	Food	175	175	175	=SUM(B13:D13)
14	Fares	55	55	55	=SUM(B14:D14)
15	Leisure	30	38	33	=SUM(B15:D15)
16	Expenditure Total	=SUM(B10:B15)	=SUM(C10:C15)	=SUM(D10:D15)	=SUM(B16:D16)
17					
18	REMAINING	=B7-B16	=C7-C16	=D7-D16	=SUM(B18:D18)

Figure 6.1 Entering personal budget details

4 Save your work using the filename **U6PB1**, and print a copy of your work.

The amount of money that you have **remaining** is referred to as the amount that can be **carried forward** to the next month. It is shown in the next month as **brought forward**. Putting in these figures gives you an idea of how long it might take you to save a particular amount of money.

Now you are going to see how to set up a budget that shows you how to carry forward the money you save each month, and include it in the next month's total.

5 You can *either* copy the details from Figure 6.2 (including the formulae) into your spreadsheet, making sure you enter the contents in the cells exactly as shown;

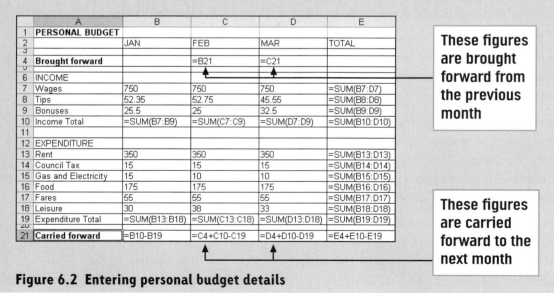

	A	B	C	D	E
1	PERSONAL BUDGET				
2		JAN	FEB	MAR	TOTAL
3					
4	Brought forward		=B21	=C21	
5					
6	INCOME				
7	Wages	750	750	750	=SUM(B7:D7)
8	Tips	52.35	52.75	45.55	=SUM(B8:D8)
9	Bonuses	25.5	25	32.5	=SUM(B9:D9)
10	Income Total	=SUM(B7:B9)	=SUM(C7:C9)	=SUM(D7:D9)	=SUM(B10:D10)
11					
12	EXPENDITURE				
13	Rent	350	350	350	=SUM(B13:D13)
14	Council Tax	15	15	15	=SUM(B14:D14)
15	Gas and Electricity	15	10	10	=SUM(B15:D15)
16	Food	175	175	175	=SUM(B16:D16)
17	Fares	55	55	55	=SUM(B17:D17)
18	Leisure	30	38	33	=SUM(B18:D18)
19	Expenditure Total	=SUM(B13:B18)	=SUM(C13:C18)	=SUM(D13:D18)	=SUM(B19:D19)
20					
21	Carried forward	=B10-B19	=C4+C10-C19	=D4+D10-D19	=E4+E10-E19

These figures are brought forward from the previous month

These figures are carried forward to the next month

Figure 6.2 Entering personal budget details

or, if you know how to insert rows into a spreadsheet, you can add additional rows into the spreadsheet from the exercise above and re-enter the formulae.

6   Save your work using the filename **U6PB2**.

7   Print a copy of your work.

▪▪▫ EVIDENCE ACTIVITIES

Create your own personal budget

1   Create your own personal budget using the example from the exercise above. Your spreadsheet should cover the next **six** months. Remove any of the items that do not apply, and add any extra items that you need. You can use the calculations you already made in the *Thinking about personal finances* activity, page 94.

2   Complete the spreadsheet.

3   Save your work using the filename **U6PB3**.

4   Print a copy of your work.

Planning from a personal budget

1   From looking at your newly completed budget, calculate how long it would take you to save for a holiday costing £300.

2   What other ways could you get the money for the holiday?

unit 7

PC systems

In this unit you see how a PC works — the purpose of the components and how to connect them. You will look at the price, quality, suitability and use. You will also write a simple user guide.

In this unit you will need to learn about:

▷ the key components of a PC system

▷ different PC systems for an end-user

▷ how to research a suitable PC for a specified end-user

▷ how to develop user guidance for a specified end-user.

Components of a PC system

Computers seem to be complicated, but they are not as difficult to understand as you might think. If you are going to work with them it is worth getting to know what the components do. A Personal Computer (PC) processes data by following sets of instructions called programs. It is made up of the following hardware:

The monitor

The monitor is also known as the screen or VDU (Visual Display Unit). You can see what you are currently doing on the PC and the results of the work carried out by the processor.

There are two types of monitor: CRT and flat panel.

• • • *CRT screens*

A CRT (Cathode Ray Tube) monitor works like a TV set: an electron gun at the back shoots electrons at coloured phosphors painted on the inside of the front glass, making them light up.

• • • *TFT screens*

Flat-panel screens have become more popular for desktop PCs. They use the same TFT (Thin Film Transistor) technology found in some laptop screens (these screens are also called active-matrix displays). Each coloured dot is a separate transistor that is turned on and off to make a picture.

Flat-panel screens take up less desk space, use less power, and the display is flicker-free. However, they are more expensive – about double the cost of a CRT of a similar size.

Input devices

Input devices are the components of a PC system that feed information into the computer to be processed. Here are some key examples:

• • • *The mouse*

This is a pointing device that enables you to select and move items on screen. There are now different types. The most common has a ball underneath it. The ball rotates as you move it, and operates two wheels inside the mouse, one for horizontal, and one for vertical movement. The mouse pointer is displayed in differing ways depending on position and function. The buttons can be used to select options.

The introduction of the mouse was an important factor in the development of visual computing – it was necessary to have a tool capable of moving to, selecting, and dragging pictures, menus and documents.

• • • *The keyboard*

This consists of keys based on the standard typewriter layout QWERTY plus additional keys, such as function keys, arrow keys, the Control (Ctrl), Alt and Shift keys.

• • • *The joystick*

This is mainly used to operate movement in computer games. Three kinds of data are sent to the computer – horizontal movement, vertical movement, and on-off signals. Those used with flight-simulator players have an extra control on the top which provides another set of thumb-operated controls. Other types of controllers are now being used – for example, driving games use steering wheels, and often have a separate foot pedal unit for accelerating and braking.

GIVE IT A GO   input devices

Can you think of any more input devices used on a PC?

Output devices

Output devices are the elements of a PC system that allow you to produce the results of instructions in some format or another. Here are some key examples:

• • • *The printer*

This is a means by which you can view your work as hard copy. Printer quality has improved enormously in recent years, while prices have continued to drop. It is more difficult today to choose between an inkjet and a laser printer because the difference in price is less and the quality of printing is closer.

Inkjet printer
These work by squirting tiny drops of ink onto paper in controlled patterns. Colour inkjets use four colours (cyan, magenta, yellow and black). There is usually a separate ink cartridge for black ink, because being used for text, it is used more than the colours.

Laser printer
These work by a laser creating an electrically charged pattern on the paper which attracts tiny particles of toner. These are then fused to the paper with heat.

• • • *The speakers*

Your computer can both produce and receive sound. Most sound cards have two toutput options: a speaker port, which

A printer with its cartridge

delivers an already-amplified signal to speakers, and a line-out port, which delivers an unamplified signal. If you have speakers, you get better sound by connecting to the line-out port and allowing the speakers to carry out the amplification.

GIVE IT A GO output devices

Can you think of any more output devices used on a PC?

Storage

Storage is where you save the data, programs or other files which you are using on your PC system. There are two main types of storage:

• • • *Internal storage*

The *hard disk drive* is the built-in storage device where you store programs and data files. Hard disk capacity has grown dramatically. Standard computer systems today have hard drives with multi-gigabyte (1024 megabytes) capacity.

• • • *Removable storage*

This allows you to save and load data, programs or other files that are not held permanently on the computer, using one or other type of *drive*. You must use the correct type of disk for the type of drive. The types of drive and disk are:

Floppy drives

These have become smaller in size and larger in capacity. The standard now is 3.5 inch with a 1.44 megabyte capacity. They are used to store relatively small files and move them from computer to computer. They store data magnetically in a series of circular bands. The disk rotates while a magnetic head moves in and out across the bands in search of the required data.

CD-ROM drives

These can hold up to 650 megabytes of data. CD drives can read CDs whether they are data CDs, storing computer data, or audio CDs that you use on your stereo. A CD-ROM stores data optically (a laser beam reads the microscopic pits in the surface of the disk).

DVD-ROM drives

These can hold 4.7 gigabytes of data. DVD drives can read CDs as well as DVD data discs and movie discs. A DVD-ROM also stores data optically.

Disk drive options gaining popularity are the CD recorder (CD-RW) and the DVD recorder (DVD-RW), drives that can not only read CDs but create them too. Most computers are sold with at least floppy and CD-ROM drives as a built-in standard, but it is usually possible to upgrade to the more advanced drives. It is also possible to buy external versions of these drives, which connect to your computer via ports.

Internal components

The 'computing' done by a computer is carried out by important components found within the processor tower, which is part of your PC system. These include:

• • • *The CPU*

The CPU (Central Processing Unit) is also known as the microprocessor. It carries out the instructions. There are different types of processor. The speed at which they perform is measured in megahertz (MHz). This is referred to as the clock speed.

Comparing performance may seem straightforward – some are bigger than others, and bigger seems to mean more speed. However, you cannot compare different kinds of processors in that way. Numbers are only comparable within a particular processor type (e.g. Pentium) since clock speed is only one factor in overall performance.

• • • *Memory*

A PC has two kinds of memory:

RAM (Random-Access Memory) is the short-term memory. Power is required to retain information. Data stored in RAM is lost when power is turned off. The greater the capacity the PC has to temporarily store instructions and data, the quicker programs will run. RAM is faster than ROM. Extra RAM needed for running big programs can easily be added if you want to upgrade the performance of your computer.

ROM (Read Only Memory) stores all permanent data such as software programs, system BIOS, sound and video cards.

• • • *The motherboard*

This is the underlying circuit board that connects all the other components. Computer parts may be soldered directly onto the board, or new circuits (called *cards*) inserted into expansion slots included on it. A computer's connecting ports (i.e. Parallel, serial, USB etc) are plugged into the motherboard.

• • • *BIOS*

The BIOS (Basic Input-Output System) is software stored on a chip that controls the way the compute r interacts with the keyboard, screen, disk drives, and serial and parallel ports.

The modem

A modem allows communication over a phone line with other computers. As a phone line transmits sound, the modem turns data into a sound pattern which the modem on the receiving

The inside of a CPU

end turns back into data. Turning it into sound is called modulation, and turning it back into data is demodulation.

Modems can be installed internally (inside the computer in an expansion slot) or externally (a separate box connected to a serial or USB port). Most computers sold today include an internal modem. They come with different speed ratings – the standard is 56 Kbps.

GIVE IT A GO   connecting the components

It is important that you know how to connect the various components of your PC system. At the back of your computer you should identify the correct sockets for the following items:

- *Keyboard*: The keyboard port can look like the mouse port. Some manufacturers now colour code cables to help you to make the correct connections.
- *Modem*: You will notice that the connector looks like a telephone connector.
- *Mouse*: If your mouse is not working, check this port – it may be that the mouse plug has come loose.
- *Printer*: This is most likely to be the parallel port – a wide connector with eight pins.

Prepare a diagram of all the connections at the back of your PC.

■■■■ EVIDENCE ACTIVITIES

Key concepts of a PC system

1   Prepare a diagram showing the components of a PC.

2   Label the diagram.

2   Explain the purpose of the main memory and other processing components of a PC system.

Identify computer parts

Using your own images, label the following computer parts:

1   **On the monitor:**

Wallpaper

Icon

Window

Power button

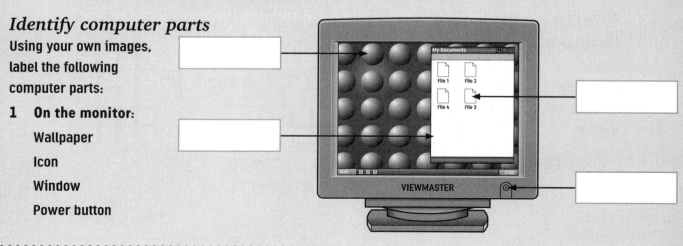

2 **On the mouse:**
Click
Right click
Scrolling button

3 **On the tower** (computer or CPU):
CD–ROM Drive
Floppy disk drive
Power button

4 **On the keyboard:**
Enter key
Escape key
Caps lock
Space bar
Arrow keys
Numeric keypad
Control, Alt,
and Delete
(Backspace)
Buttons

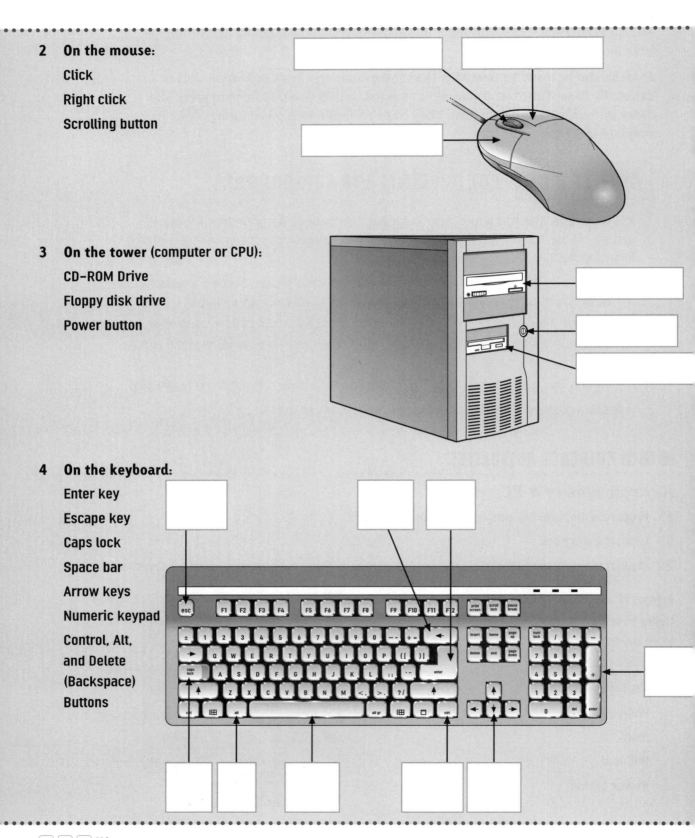

Different PC systems for an end-user

Computers carry out sets of instructions to perform many of the tasks that were previously carried out manually. In the last twenty years the power of PCs, and the number of devices that can be attached to them has grown enormously. They are now commonly used in all kinds of business. Using a PC increases speed, accuracy and can improve productivity.

GIVE IT A GO   the advantages of the PC

1   Think of three tasks that might be carried out in a business.
2   Explain why you think these tasks would be more efficiently carried out on a PC.

The operating system

The programs that run the PC are called system software. An operating system ensures that all parts of the computer system work together. It controls the hardware and starts and operates the software. It provides ways to manage files stored on the computer.

Windows is the name of a series of operating systems from Microsoft. Early versions were targeted at low-end home PCs, but more recent versions have begun tackling the server market. Windows is the most commonly used operating system.

Application software

Certain software, such as word processing, spreadsheet, database and presentation programs are used, mainly, to carry out routine tasks within an organisation. They are all examples of application software. Other applications used to carry out functions that all businesses have to do, regardless of the product or service, include:

● ● ● *Payroll software*

This software is used to automate paying employees. It saves time, simplifies the process and ensures accuracy. It allows a company to automate year-end routines, calculate TAX, National Insurance and net pay. It can also produce detailed pay slips and management reports. Tax year-end processing produces all the required payroll reports and year-end reports in the format acceptable by Inland Revenue. It must comply with the latest government legislation.

● ● ● *HR software*

Human resources software is used for managing staff and optimising human resources. It can be used in conjunction with payroll software. Fast and easy access to personnel records saves time and improves the usefulness of employee information.

GIVE IT A GO   research application software

1   Find out what programs the latest version of Microsoft Office includes.
2   Briefly explain what each of the programs can do.

Specialist software

If you work in a specialist field you will almost certainly require specialist software to carry out your job.

● ● ● *Accounts software*

This software is designed to speed up the time-consuming task of bookkeeping and accounting. The programs calculate the figures for VAT returns, produce invoices, track cash-flow and manage payment and receipts.

● ● ● *Travel agency software*

Travel agents require software that will permit:

- searches on location and cost
- on-line booking
- additional customer options, such as extra nights
- access to a large number of holidays, flights, and other services such as car hire
- the same services available in the high street and on-line.

● ● ● *Web design software*

Web designers will probably want software with the ability to:

- organise the components and build a website
- make master templates for page uniformity
- create, edit and animate graphics
- add interactive elements, pop-up menus and buttons
- add effects
- keep track of updates to any page element
- keep track of who did what, to what part of the site, for sites that are worked on by a team.

The designer may also need to provide a website that includes *E-commerce* software. This enables selling on-line easily and (more importantly) securely. It allows sales, has customer accounting and price options. It can be linked to product information in another application to allow changes to be automatically published to the website.

● ● ● *CAD and CAM software*

CAD and CAM (Computer Aided Design; Computer Aided Manufacture) software provides everything required to go from the design to the end product. It allows the company to evaluate more design alternatives, reduce errors, and improve product quality.

The software allows the creation of 3D models from 2D data. You may have seen the use of this software, for example, in designing a kitchen installation.

Computer Aided Manufacture allows computers to drive machinery. Human intervention may well be required in the process.

● ● ● *Graphics software*

The design industry requires specialist software across all forms of media. This type of package would be used by designers, but is also now being used more by individuals interested in digital imagery. The software provides the following functions:

- industry standard for photographers and web and graphic designers
- advanced tools for photo editing (red eye removal, auto-colour correction, etc.)
- simulation of painting techniques
- large effects library
- automatically builds photo galleries that can be published on the web.

Research a suitable PC for a specified end-user

Which system should you recommend for a specific user? The system must be the right price as well as meeting the needs of the business. It is not a good idea to focus on price as this can be ineffective and unproductive. Whatever the system, there may be a need to adjust some of the requirements.

To make a decision about recommending a system, you should consider:

- Who is going to use it?
- What type of business is it for?
- What is it going to be used for?
- What type of software will be required?
- What type of devices, and how many will be required?
- Will the user need further expansion?
- How much money is available to spend?
- Does the user have a preference for a type of hardware and/or software? For example, do they require a desktop or a laptop, what peripheral devices, such as printers, scanners, speakers or cameras do they require, what size and type of monitor do they want?

Do your research

You should make sure that you know what is available. You can read reviews in computer magazines and there are many websites that have lists of machines with accompanying reviews. Reading reviews is a good way of getting to know the standard terms and common specifications.

You must read the specifications, and if you are not sure of, or do not know, the meaning you can get information from a message board or a technical glossary on the Internet.

Write down the criteria

When you have read some reviews you will begin to get a general feel for which details matter and which do not.

For example, nearly all PCs now have 56K modems, so although a modem is a factor, because most PCs all have this feature, you would not base your decision on it. Decision-making factors would probably include, for example, processor speed, available ports, screen size, and battery life for laptops.

Write down the criteria that matter most to the proposed user so that you can draw up a priorities list. You can then decide which systems meet your criteria when you compare them.

You will see that there are a lot of systems that meet your criteria. You may decide to buy one PC instead of another, simply because you prefer black to grey. This is fine as long as both systems meet your *significant* criteria. There are many good, affordable systems that allow a freedom of choice previously unavailable.

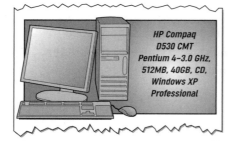

HP Compaq
D530 CMT
Pentium 4–3.0 GHz,
512MB, 40GB, CD,
Windows XP
Professional

NEC Powermate
ML6 Slimtine
Pentium 4, 2.8 GHz,
256MB, 80GB,
DVD/CDRW,
FDD, NIC, Windows XP
Professional, 3-year
onsite warranty

You will need to research to find out which computer is right for the user

Different types of user

Here are some of the different types of user and their requirements. Thinking about the user will help you know what criteria matter when you are choosing a PC system to recommend to them.

● ● ● *Accountants*

These require specialist software to meet the requirements of their clients. There is a range of accounting, payroll and other software. Regardless of the size of the business – from small businesses to multinationals, the software must meet the client needs and the tax regulations and employment laws in the country where they are being submitted.

• • • *Travel agents*

These, like any other business, want systems that make the process of planning and booking a holiday package more efficient and provide good customer service so that they compete with the ever-growing competition.

Because hotels, resorts and airlines now use the Internet to advertise their services themselves, and allow customers to book direct (often at reduced rates), the travel agent is constantly seeking new ways to increase the value of their service to attract clients and increase profits.

• • • *Web designers*

These may in the past have created websites using only code – HTML or JavaScript. Software is now available that allows website development and the creation of web graphics. The designer wants the most efficient way to create websites. Most programs use visual page layouts, although the designer can also still use code.

• • • *Teachers*

A few examples of software that teachers may want to use include:

- software about the subject itself, designed for whole class or individual use
- software that allows linking with other schools around the world. Each school studies the same topic, and they then share the results. This can be particularly useful for foreign languages and multicultural awareness
- software to assist in administration and preparation such as:
  - creating exams and tests and marking them
  - creating comments for reports
  - creating lesson plans and assignments.

• • • *Secretaries*

These are responsible for a variety of administrative and clerical duties required to run and maintain an office. No only do they use many types of office machines and equipment including photocopiers and telephone systems, they now use PCs for an increasing amount of their work.

All secretaries must be familiar with the language, forms and procedures in the business in which they are working. Some will be required to carry out specialised work, for say, engineers, solicitors or scientists. In these jobs knowledge of technical terms and procedures is essential, for example a *legal secretary* will have to know how to prepare legal papers such as summonses, complaints and other court documents.

Today, secretaries use PCs to run spreadsheet, word processing, database management, desktop publishing, graphics and other programs. They will probably be using integrated software packages such as Microsoft Office.

◼◼◼ EVIDENCE ACTIVITIES

Choosing a PC system for an end-user

1 List the *hardware* and *software* that you think each of the following may require to provide a useful system to carry out their job: Accountant, Secretary, Travel Agent, Web Designer, Teacher, Writer.

2 Using magazine and/or Internet reviews, choose systems for each of these users. Make sure the specifications meet the requirements of each end-user.

3 Explain why you have chosen those systems for each of the users.

PC solutions for common office tasks

Decide which of the programs in Microsoft Office you think would be best to carry out each of these tasks:

▢ arrange meetings and appointments

▢ check for correct spelling and grammar

▢ petty cash

▢ prepare meetings agendas

▢ prepare pages for publication on the web

▢ produce a letter to all your customers

▢ prepare a slide show for a forthcoming exhibition

▢ update customer records

▢ prepare a four-page brochure giving details of your latest products including images of the products

▢ keep track of the daily work

▢ produce reports.

Training needs

If a company or user is to get the full benefit of the software and hardware they are buying and using, they need to understand how to use it fully.

A great deal of the software that is used for a specific purpose, such as payroll or CAD/CAM will require the user to understand the 'manual' processes involved. Using the software is a quick, easy and reliable way of carrying out those processes.

Training needs are often overlooked, and this can result in inefficient use of systems. Computer training is itself a large field, and covers all aspects of IT. The training may be carried out by, for example, the product manufacturer, a specialist training company, or by an educational establishment.

GIVE IT A GO training courses

1   Find three establishments that provide training for Microsoft Office.
2   Compare the courses, and draw up a table of your findings including:
   - course content
   - cost
   - length of course
   - qualification, if any, at the end of the course.

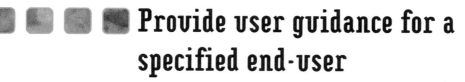

Provide user guidance for a specified end-user

Preparing a guide

You have to outline what the user needs to know to set up and use equipment. Keep it simple, cover the basics, and use language the user will understand. You should bear in mind the level of knowledge and experience they have about PC systems.

You may find it helpful to use screen shots to illustrate your guide (see Producing a screen shot in the Introduction, page ix).

You may find it useful to try out your guide on a friend who does not know about PCs. This will help you to see where your instructions are not be clear enough.

You may want to include the following items in your guide:

● ● ● *Introduction*

The guide should begin with an introduction, in which you may include:

- *Why use a computer?*: explain the advantages such as (for example) speed, accuracy and the ability to access the Internet, and to use images, video and sound. You should also specify the advantages for the specific user's job.
- *How to use Help*: explain that the user can get on-line assistance while working, and how to do this.
- *Use of tutorials*: there are often on-line tutorials to help the user. In *your* guide you should encourage use of them.

• • • *Setting up a PC*

You may then want to include this type of item in your guide:

- *Before you begin*: List the components and give a brief explanation of their use. (You prepared this type of information in the *Key concepts of a PC system* exercise on page 111). Advise the user to check the connections for each component, and explain the connections.
- *Setting up your PC*: Explain how to put the components together. Give simple instructions on how to do it, such as:

To set up your PC

1) Connect the equipment together using the diagram shown.
2) Plug the power cords into the power supply following the manufacturer's instructions.
3) Press the power buttons of your PC, the monitor and any additional devices to the **ON** position.

• • • *Desktop skills*

Depending on the level of ability of the user, you may need to include these items in your guide:

- How to use the equipment (such as the mouse: understand when to click, double-click or right click; how to drag and drop).
- How to start the computer up.
- How to log on.
- How to load a program (how to locate and open a program using icons using the **start** menu).
- The parts of a program window (the title, tool, menu and scroll bars).
- How to locate and open files.
- How to save files using the correct file type. You may want to give the most common file extensions, such as:
  - Graphic files   .bmp, .gif, .tif, .jpg
  - Word document files   .doc
  - Web pages files   .htm, (html)
  - Unformatted text files   .txt
  - Excel spreadsheet files   .xls
- How to use the Internet:
  - How to connect.
  - How to create an Internet account.
  - How to set up email and messaging.
  - How to access information using a specific URL, by searching, or using a bookmark.

- How to print.
- How to exit from a program and close down the PC.

• • • *Other knowledge*

You may also include items such as:

- *Maintenance*: Explain how to take proper care of parts of a PC (floppy disks, CDs, etc.).
- *Security*: Explain use of anti-virus software.
- *Housekeeping*: Explain the need for making backups of program and data files.
- *Problem solving*: (Also known as trouble-shooting.) Explain diagnosis and correction of minor or common problems. This is an example of what you may want to provide:

Problem	You do not want to print a file you have sent to the printer.
Solution	Check the print queue, select the job and delete it: 1 Locate the printer icon at the bottom right of the screen (near the time). 2 Click it to open the window that lists the print jobs. The status of each job will be shown. 3 To delete a job, click it once to highlight it. 4 Press the delete key on your keyboard.

- *Training*: You may want to provide information on the training that is available, including the cost. (You investigated this type of information in the *training courses* activity on page 119.)

■■● EVIDENCE ACTIVITIES

Creating guidance for a specified end-user

Experienced user:

You have been asked by an engineering company that uses advanced graphical software to select a *new* PC system that will be used for running the day-to-day business. There are three members of staff using the current system. They are fairly experienced at using computers.

1   Select a suitable system.

2   Prepare user guidance to help them to set up and start using the equipment.

Inexperienced user:

You have been asked to select a PC system by a company that installs kitchens and bedroom furniture. They currently use manufacturers' advertising leaflets to show customers the products available, and prepare the designs and costings on paper. They are all inexperienced at using computers.

1   Select a suitable system.

2   Prepare user guidance to help them to set up and start using the equipment.

Benefits for your end-user

Using the system that you selected in the activity above:

1   Explain why you selected the system you have suggested — the hardware and software.

2   Explain the benefits that the company will get from using the system you have chosen.

unit 8

Using the Internet

This unit has been designed to help you to learn how to use the Internet. You will practice using email to send, receive and forward mail. You will become familiar with the terms, practices and use of the Internet, including using search engines to access information.

In this unit you will need to learn about:

▸ how to use the Internet responsibly

▸ how to send, receive and forward emails

▸ how to search, explore, visit and bookmark a range of websites

▸ how to select and save information from websites for use in other applications.

Note: in this unit the Internet Service Provider is AOL, using Broadband. What you see on your screen will differ depending on your ISP, and also on the version of the program that you are running. Any pages you access may have been updated since the publication of this book, and so may not look exactly the same as the figures shown.

Using the Internet

How it works

To use the Internet you need to use electronic communication software – a package that allows you to communicate with computers and people all over the world. You can exchange emails, search for information, research, and buy and sell goods or services. Data is sent between the computers via communication lines. To transfer the data you need a modulator-demodulator (*modem*), which is a device that converts a digital signal generated by a computer into an analogue signal which can be transmitted along a telephone line.

The World Wide Web is a network of computers across the globe which communicate with each other via the telephone lines. A website is a page or pages on the World Wide Web belonging to an organisation, company or an individual. The first page is called the *home page*. Web pages are written using *HTML* (HyperText Markup Language) to describe the contents and appearance of elements on a page, such as paragraph, table, or image.

• • • 'Surfing the net'

You can 'surf' the World Wide Web using automatic links called *hyperlinks*. A hyperlink is a way of getting from one page to another destination without having to enter another address. You may also move to a different location on the same page (a picture, an email address or a program). You can use *search engines* – programs that enable you to search the Internet by keywords or topics – to carry out searches and locate websites. You can gather data, store web addresses, save and print data. You should be very careful about downloading data from the Internet as it is a source of viruses (programs that can infect your PC and destroy programs and data on it).

A *web browser* is software that allows you to view, navigate and interact with the World Wide Web. There are a number of browsers available, and there are differences between them, but they all carry out the same functions.

Website addresses

To log on to a website you must know the address. Every web page has a unique address. This is known as the *URL* (Uniform Resource Locator). A URL would normally start with '**http://www.**'. The letters http represent HyperText Transfer Protocol – the instruction to the browser to look for a web page.

A web address will also include the domain name, the organisation's name, and the type of site:

.co	a company or commercial organisation in the UK
.com	a company or commercial organisation
.ac	an academic community in the UK
.edu	an educational institution
.org	a non-profit organisation
.uk	is the country. Each country has a unique code. If no code is shown it (usually) indicates an American site

The dots are important in a web address and the address must be 100 per cent correct or it will not reach its destination.

Setting up an Internet account

• • • *Choosing a provider*

In order to use the Internet you will have to choose an *ISP* (Internet Service Provider). ISPs charge you for the use of a telephone number that will connect you to the Internet via their servers. They 'host' your email account, which means they store emails from you on their servers until the person you have emailed to goes on-line, and vice versa. Each provider offer a range of 'hosting' services (e.g. email, web space, chat room, message boards, shopping links). The packages range from simple dial-up, to broadband network connection.

• • • *Internet charges*

Most ISPs will provide the software that you require free of charge. This will be their own software, or well-known alternatives such as Microsoft Internet Explorer or Netscape Explorer. Charging practices vary, for example, you may pay a monthly all-inclusive flat rate or pay as you go and a limited rental fee. Don't forget that some ISP fees do not include the cost of the telephone call! The deal you choose may depend on how much time you think you are likely to spend on-line. Providers may also offer free hardware, for example, a free modem if you use their broadband service.

• • • *Setting up and accessing an account*

Once you have chosen your provider you must then set up an account. Most PC systems have an automatic setup program to configure your computer to access the Internet via your chosen ISP. In order to use your account you will have to log on using your password. Most PC systems allow for automatic entry of your password so that you do not have to remember and re-enter it each time. Once you have done this, you are ready to access the web.

choosing a service provider

1 Investigate three service providers.
2 Compare the services they provide (include the equipment required, costs, and levels of service including broadband).

Accessing a website

To display a web page enter the web address in the address box and press **Enter** or click on the **Go** (or equivalent) button.

The first page of the website is displayed. It is quicker to load a web page when you do not load the images as they are large files. You can set up your browser so that it does not display images.

You should be careful about the type of website that you access and you should not disclose personal information.

Using hyperlinks

When you have accessed a website you click on the hyperlinks to take you to other pages within the current site (or to other websites). Links can take the form of underlined text, text in a different font colour, or they can be image links.

Toolbar buttons

Toolbar buttons are provided for you to move around the software. Remember the same functions will be provided no matter which service provider you use, but they will look different.

Service providers include these functions:

Back	to view the page you looked at before the page currently displayed
Forward	to view the page you looked at before you used the Back button
Refresh	use if a page does not seem to be loading properly
Stop	use if the page you are trying to load is taking too long to load
Home	to load your home page
Search	to allow you to search the Internet
Favourites	to display a list of site addresses you have stored – allowing you to add to the list
History	to list the sites you have visited, so you can view them offline

GIVE IT A GO   *enter a website*

1   Load your software and enter your account using your password.
2   Enter the address: **www.hmso.gov.uk**. The home page of the site will be displayed.

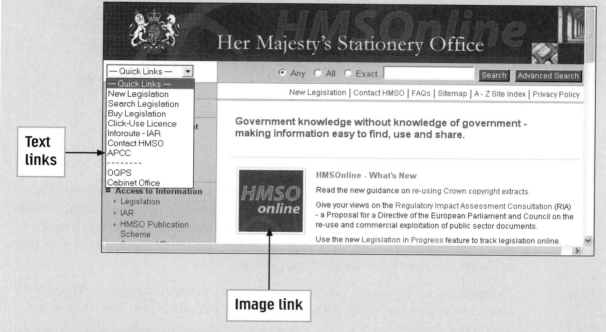

Figure 8.1 HMSO Online home page

3   Move down the screen until you see the Most Requested Acts section, and load the Data Protection Act 1998.

4   Look at the Act.
5   Exit the site.

Figure 8.2 Most Requested Acts

**Figure 8.3
AOL toolbar buttons**

The toolbar buttons for Internet Explorer look like this:

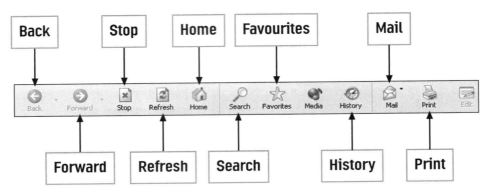

Figure 8.4 Internet Explorer toolbar buttons

Hotmail

MSN Hotmail is free, web-based email (which means you don't need a specific computer with the right set up to access your account). You can read and receive emails. It is useful for people who use more than one computer, travel frequently, or do not own a computer. Messages are stored in a central location, so your Inbox is always up to date, no matter where you are.

To send and receive email you go to the Hotmail website and sign in. You can do this anywhere in the world. Although the basic account is free, you can pay for additional services.

GIVE IT A GO   set up a Hotmail account

Create a Hotmail account by going to the sign-in page **www.hotmail.com**. Click on the New Account Sign Up tab, and follow the instructions.

■■■■ EVIDENCE ACTIVITY

Setting up on the Internet: user-guide

Describe stage-by-stage the process of setting up an Internet/email account for a beginner who wishes to start using the Internet. (See Unit 7, pages 119–121 for an example of how to produce a user guide.)

Keeping yourself safe

The Internet allows you access to all kinds of information around the world. It has changed how we communicate, how businesses operate and how we conduct our lives. It has given us a virtual playground, an international school and a place to meet and make friends. But like any technology, it can be abused.

●●● *Chat rooms*

Internet chat rooms allow people to have conversations which are typed, rather than spoken, about common interests such as music or sport. As you type, the message can be seen instantaneously by everyone else using the chat room.

The first rule of chat rooms is NEVER to reveal any personal details – that includes full name, address, telephone number, email address and mobile number.

To monitor use of a screen name, you can use facilities provided by the service provider, such as:

- *Activity reports*: each time the screen name is used an email is sent giving, for example, the websites visited and the number of emails sent.
- *Timers*: these allow you to limit the amount of time spent on-line. You can control the number of hours as well as specifying the hours, for example, between 16:00 and 20:00.

GIVE IT A GO purchasing on-line

1   Name products and services you would purchase using the Internet.
2   Name products that you would not choose to buy over the Internet and explain why.
3   What website would you trust to buy things from, and why?

  # Send, receive and forward emails

Using email allows you to send and receive messages from friends, family and companies around the world, and from business colleagues at your own site, or at other sites nationally and internationally. You can copy and forward messages to other people or groups of people.

Using your email account

Before you can use email you must load the appropriate software on your system and set up an account for your use.

Load the program by going to the **start** button and selecting it from the **All Programs** menu, or if one is available, use your shortcut icon. Enter any passwords required to gain access to your account. Most programs will have folders where incoming messages are stored, where outgoing messages are stored and where sent messages are stored

Sending messages

You can prepare your email messages on-line (connected to the phone line and therefore incurring charges) or off-line (not connected to the phone line and therefore not incurring phone costs). If you are charged by the amount of time you are on-line it is better to prepare your messages off-line as it will cost less.

It is vital that you enter the address with 100 per cent accuracy or it will not reach its destination. Each dot (full stop) is important. Check the address once you have entered it and if you have made an error, correct it. Email addresses are made up of:

- the user's name
- followed by the @ symbol
- followed by the address of the user's service provider which includes the domain.

You should check your email content carefully to ensure that it contains the information you want to send. Most systems have a spell-checking facility built in.

You may have a picture, data or a file that you want to send with your message. If you add any such file to an email it is called an attachment. You can add as many attachments as you choose. These are often condensed (or zipped) for speed of transmission and you need to unzip the files before use. Mail and attachments can be printed.

To transmit the message that you have prepared click on the **Send Now** button. The message will be sent automatically and when the transmission is completed a message will be displayed. You can also choose to send the message at a later point. When it has been transmitted, it is placed in **Sent Email** folder.

▨▨▨ EVIDENCE ACTIVITY

Sending an email

Create the message shown below and send it to someone who you know has an email address. When you have entered the message check the spelling and, in particular, check that you have keyed in the address correctly.

To	[Insert person's email address]
Subject	Email evidence

[insert person's name]

As I am just beginning to use email, I would be grateful if you would reply to this message so that I can provide evidence that I have:

- sent this message
- opened and printed your reply.

Thanks.

[insert your name]

Copying messages

You can send the same message to more than one address:

• • • *Sending the message on equal terms*

Enter the email addresses in the **Send to** box, inserting a comma between, for example:

M.Jackson@serviceprovider.co.uk,L.Cave@serviceprovider.ac.uk

• • • *Sending 'carbon copies'*

Enter the email address of the main recipient in the **To** box. Enter the second email address in the **Copy to** box. You may send a copy to more than one person.

You can also send 'blind' copies – i.e. send a copy to a third party without the main recipient knowing.

▣▣▣ EVIDENCE ACTIVITY

Sending an email copy

Send the following message to someone you know and a copy to your tutor. The subject of the message should be: Activity 2

> [insert person's name]
>
> This exercise is to demonstrate the use of the copy facility.
>
> [insert your name

Opening received mail messages

When you have loaded your email program, it will notify you if you have received any email. Email always identifies the sender, and usually gives the date and time the message was sent.

Be careful when opening email as this is a way of spreading viruses. Your system will normally issue warnings regarding opening mail and attachments. A disadvantage of using email is the amount of unsolicited mail that can be sent to you. This is called SPAM, and is like junk mail.

To open any messages you have received go to the message and either double-click on it, or use the commands. You do not have to open any messages if you do not recognise the source, and you should never download data if this is the case.

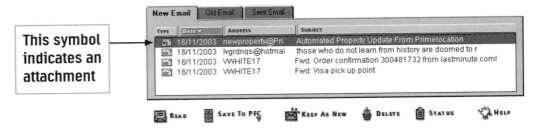

Figure 8.5 Opening received messages

Once you have opened one of the messages you will see these commands at the foot of the screen.

Figure 8.6 Options once mail is opened

You can move to the next message (without having to return to the original screen), delete the message or save it.

The options for storing the message are:

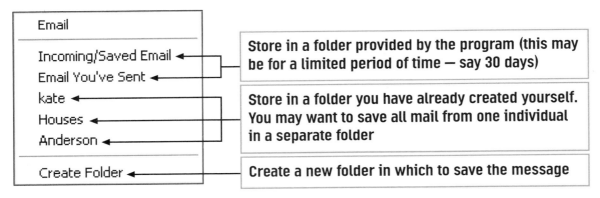

Figure 8.7 Options for storing messages

Replying to a message

To send a reply to a message it must be open. Then, click on the **Reply** button. As the address and subject are already entered, you just need to enter your reply. You can then send the message in the normal manner.

If there are many email addresses on the original message and you want to reply to all of them, click on the **Reply All**.

If you want to send a copy of the message to a new recipient click on the **Forward** button. Enter the email address of the new person or group. You can also add your own message to the one that you are forwarding.

Keeping your system safe

One of the main concerns about using emails is that it can allow your system to become infected by:

- *Viruses*: pieces of software that cause unexpected, usually bad, events. They are often disguised as document files, games or images.
- *Worms*: viruses that reside in the computer memory and replicate or copy themselves. They may send such copies to other computers, including by email.
- *Trojans*: programs that pretend to be a good application, but do things that you do not expect. They are not viruses as they do not replicate, but they can be just as destructive.

Firewall software helps to protect against unwanted access. It can deny access to unauthorised programs such as trojans. However, it is not impregnable, and only when used with anti-virus software can it provide a basic level of protection.

The address book

The address book enables you to store addresses you use often. Using the Address book means that you do not have to remember or re-key email addresses.

• • • *Adding an address*

To add an address to the address book, you click on the **Address Book** button. Your address book is displayed:

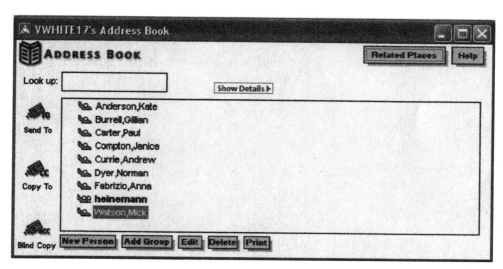

Figure 8.8 Displaying your address book

Click on the **New Person** button and the **Contact Details** dialogue box is displayed. Enter the details of someone whose email address you know, and click on **Save**.

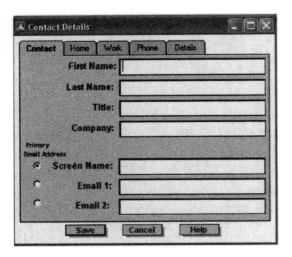

Figure 8.9 The Contact Details dialogue box

You can add addresses to your address book when you receive an email. To do so, open the email message that contains the name that you want to add to your address book. Click on the **Add Name** button. When the **Contact Details** dialogue box is displayed, the email address will already be shown. Enter the remaining details then click on **Save**.

▣▣▣ EVIDENCE ACTIVITY

Setting up an address book

Add at least five addresses to your address book (preferably the members of the group following this course). Produce screen shots of your address book both before and after your additions, and keep these in your evidence folder.

● ● ● *Adding a group*

To send the same message to a group of people, rather than enter all the addresses, or send copies, you can create a group. By entering the name of the group, you send the message to all the members in it.

To do this, click on the **Address Book** button. Your address book is displayed. Click on the **Add Group** button. The **Manage Group** dialogue box is displayed.

Enter a name for the group. Select from the names in your address book and click on the **NEW PERSON** button to add each member of the group.

When you have entered all the contacts into the group, click on the **Save** button.

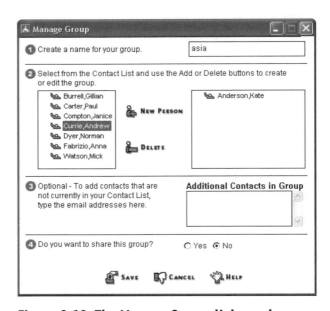

Figure 8.10 The Manage Group dialogue box

• • • *Deleting an address*

Open your address book and highlight the address (or group) that you want to delete. Click on the **Delete** button. Click on **Yes** when asked to confirm the delete.

▣▣▣ EVIDENCE ACTIVITIES

Setting up an email group

1   Add the following contact to your address book: Jan.Compton@anywhere.com

2   Delete one of the names in your address book.

3   Set up a new group called **chess**. Include Jan Compton and two other contacts in your address book.

4   Send this message to the **chess** group — the subject is **County competition**.

> If you wish to attend the competition, which is to be held in Chester on 4 February, please make sure that you inform Maura Lucking by the end of this month.

Making a presentation

Make a short presentation called 'A User Guide for Email Beginners' to demonstrate the use of email facilities to a small group of beginner–users.

You can use screen shots from your program to help (see Introduction, page ix, for instructions).

Guidelines for preparing and delivery of presentations are given in Unit 9, pages 165–170.

Search, explore, visit and bookmark a range of websites

Searching and exploring

Searching for information can be daunting. Search engines, directories and other databases have steadily improved and provide an excellent way for you to locate websites and information.

Learning about the different ways to search will provide you with better information on where to search, and help you to understand the different ways to conduct a search to find exactly what you are looking for.

• • • *Search Engines*

You cannot truly search the World Wide Web. It is made up of billions of documents and there is simply no way for your PC to find or visit them directly.

Even computers designed for this task are unable to find and index every web page. What you can do is go to a website that is designed to search for pages one at a time and collect them so that you can access them.

In other words – you can visit a search engine. They are designed to make surfing the web quick and easy. They gather information, store it in a database, and allow you to access a list of pages based on a word, or set of words.

• • • *Spiders*

Search engines work by using a program known as a *spider* or *robot*. It searches the web with a text-only browser. It reads and stores the text because that is what indicates the topic or topics on the page. The spider visits a single page and saves the text, then looks for a link to another page, where it starts the process again. Search engines are able to find and index far more web pages than you could in a lifetime of surfing.

The spiders begin their searches at websites known as directories – large websites that contain lists of links. There are millions of web pages that do not have any links from other sites and without these links, the spiders are unable to find and index them.

Search engines focus on the text content of a web page when determining where and how to rank it in the search results. They have criteria to decide which pages to display – they may look at the title of the page, the text of the page, or how many other websites link to the page.

CASE STUDY | exploring the web

A person searches for *french holidays* on AOL. As AOL uses Google to search, it sends a message to Google asking for a list of web pages to do with *french holidays*. Google then looks through its database for pages that mention *french holidays* within the site text.

Google calculates how often the phrase *french holidays* is used on the page. It also looks for other sites about *french* and/or *holidays* and counts each link from them. The pages are then ranked in the order thought to be the most relevant to the phrase *french holidays*. The list is returned to AOL, who then present it to the searcher.

Despite their usefulness, search engines are not intelligent. They are simply a series of computer programs that find and save files at a rate faster than you could.

• • • *Popular search engines*

- *Google*: This is currently the most popular search engine. It has a very large database, but it is very easy to get buried in results. It allows searches in 35 languages.

- *AlltheWeb*: This is one of the largest search sites – over two billion web pages; hundreds of millions of multimedia files; video files and software downloads. It allows searches in 49 languages.
- *AltaVista*: This used to be one of the most powerful and popular search engines. In 2003 it was bought by Overture, which was later purchased by Yahoo! It has an image and an audio/video search. It allows searches in 25 languages.
- *MSN Search*: This serves as the search engine for Microsoft's Internet access services. It allows searches in 14 languages. The search results are a combination of results from several different providers and are broken down into popular topics.

• • • *Search options*

These search engines all operate in a similar way, but have slight variations. For example:

Keywords

All the search engines **only** return search results that have ALL the keywords you have used. The order of the keywords has an impact on the results, so place the most important first.

Stop words

Google and MSN ignore common stop words such as the, is, an, who. AlltheWeb recognises them and will rewrite queries in an attempt to provide more accurate results. Altavista has a database of stop words, but discards them unless the search phrase is surrounded by quotes. MSN will include them in a query that contains other words.

Case

Google and AlltheWeb will accept words that are all lowercase, all uppercase, or a mixture of the two, and will treat them all the same – the results will not change. Using AltaVista you can also search for words that are, for example, capitalised or all lowercase by surrounding the word with quotes.

Using MSN, there is case sensitivity on specialised searches – if a query has one or more capital letters in the middle of a word, the search will look for an exact match to that combination of letters.

Stemming

None of the engines support stemming of words. For example, if you search for airline you will not find the same results as you will if you search for airlines. It is worth searching both ways. However, on AltaVista you can enter any word of three letters or more followed by a * and it will produce a search for words that begin with those three letters. Stemming can be activated on the advanced search page on MSN.

Safe search

Safe search is designed to provide a family friendly search option that eliminates listings for adult sites and other explicit content and is provided by AlltheWeb, Google and AltaVista.

Operators

Google, AlltheWeb and MSN all support a number of operators – query words that have special meaning to the search engine. By including them you can customise the search results. These operators modify the search or produce a different type of search. For instance, 'link:' is a special operator, and the query [link:www.google.com] doesn't do a normal search but instead finds all web pages that have links to www.google.com.

Several of the more common operators use punctuation instead of words, or do not require a colon. Among these operators are OR, "" (the quote operator), − (the minus operator) and + (the plus operator).

File formats

Google will narrow results to provide only specific file formats including PDF, Microsoft Word, Microsoft PowerPoint and others. AlltheWeb can also be set to either include or exclude media types like audio files and video files. AltaVista Results can be narrowed to show only HTML or PDF files. The audio/video search allows for multiple file types to be searched. MSN can also be set to either include or exclude certain media types like audio files and video files.

Time/Date

Google can limit results to pages that have been updated at specific times. AlltheWeb results can be limited to pages that have been updated within a certain time frame – you need only select *before* or *after* and enter a date. AltaVista Results can be limited to pages that have been updated within a certain time frame.

Meta-search engines

A meta-search engine allows you to visit one site, conduct a search, and view the results from a number of search engines on one results page. They do not create or maintain their own index but pass your query on to other search engines and combine the results for you. The disadvantage is that meta-search engines can produce huge quantities of information that are difficult to sift through. However, there are several reasons why you might want to use a meta-search engine:

• It is the quickest way to see the results of a variety of search engines.
• If your topic is obscure, at least one of the engines may have a result.
• Learning to use the advanced features of many search engines may take time. Meta-search engines also have advanced search functions, which means you can learn one set of commands and still search a number of engines.

The most popular are Vivisimo, DogPile, KartOO, Ixquick and Ithaki.

• • • *Directories*

Directories are databases of selected, reviewed sites arranged into categories. They include Yahoo!, Looksmart and DMOZ (which acts as the Google directory). They are previewed by editors who check to make sure that a site is active, contains unique content, and that you can actually find your way around it.

A directory nearly always contains regional categories. For example, if you are looking for an estate agent in your area, it will locate multiple, relevant listings so that you do not have to sort through pages of search engine results. Directories are also organised by topic. Browsing a directory should provide you with a list of sites that cover the exact topic you are looking for.

The logical way to navigate a directory is to browse it – read through category names and click through the listings until you find the most appropriate category.

GIVE IT A GO   compare search engines

1   Select one search engine and at least two of the meta-search engines.
2   On each of them search for **fancy dress costumes**.
3   Compare the results – include the number of results returned, the design and the links.
4   Which search engine did you find the easiest to use, and why?

• • • *The invisible web*

The visible web is content that can be indexed and searched by search engines. The invisible web consists of files, images and websites that cannot be indexed.

In late 2000 a study suggested that the portion of the web that could not be indexed was 500 times larger than the portion that could. The number of documents that have not been indexed may be around 550 billion – there are about one billion on the visible web. Web pages may not have been indexed because they cannot be accessed. This may be because the spiders could not type queries, select from form options, or enter a username and password to access the page.

▨▨▨ EVIDENCE ACTIVITIES

Search for and explore a website

1   **Log on to the Internet. In the search box, enter Acts of parliament. Any sites including these keywords will be displayed. To select any of the sites, double-click on it.**

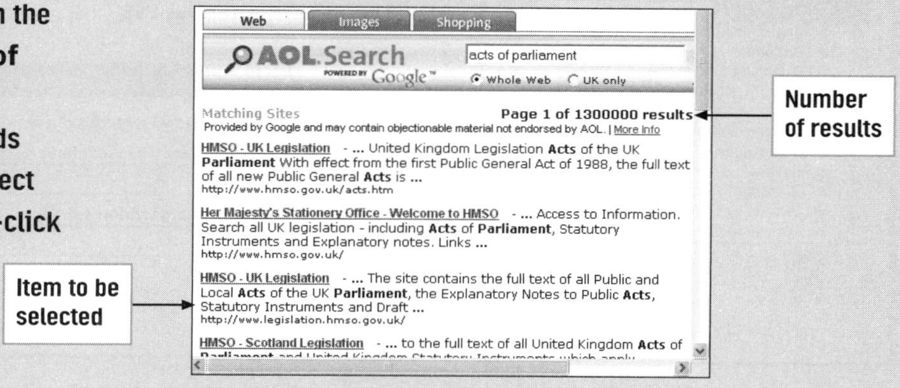

Item to be selected

Number of results

Figure 8.11 Search results

2 Select the item showing the address: www.hmso.gov.uk. The home page of the site will be displayed. This is the same website that you used before.

3 Using the hyperlinks, see if you can find out anything about the Computer Misuse Act.

4 Print the relevant pages and keep them in your evidence folder.

Compare websites

1 You have been asked to provide information about websites belonging to leisure clubs in your area.

2 Compare the sites as you find them — time taken, ease of use, helpfulness of site, useful links, etc.

3 Prepare a report comparing the sites, including a few images, and print out each of the home pages. Use the headings: Content, Design, Usability and Links.

Another reason is that some pages created by a search are dynamic; rather than someone designing that page and placing the content, the information is gathered from a variety of sources and placed on a page that is built just before you see it. These pages exist ONLY when you enter the query, and the information may change each time. This makes it impossible for a search engine to find the page or to identify the page content.

Bookmarking

When you find a site that you would like to visit again, or a site that you visit often, it is a good idea to store the address to make it easier to re-visit. Storing an address in this way is called bookmarking. A bookmark is a location, or selected text on a page, that you have marked so that you can return to it (also known as **Favourites**).

To access a favourite site, select the website name from the drop-down menu that is displayed when you select the **Favourites** menu.

To add a new favourite website, first go to the site, then select the **Favourites** menu.

From the **Favourite Places** dialogue box, select **New**. The **Add New Folder/Favourite Place** dialogue box is displayed. Enter the details and click on **OK**.

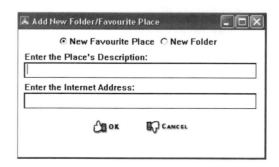

Figure 8.12 Favourite Places dialogue box

Figure 8.13 Add New Folder/Favourite dialogue box

▭▭▭ EVIDENCE ACTIVITY

Bookmarking a website

1   Log on to the Internet and bookmark the Heinemann website: **www.heinemann.com.**

2   Produce a screen shot to show the bookmarked site, and keep it in your evidence folder.

Select and save information

• • • *Saving text and/or graphics*

If you want to print information you can either make a 'hard' copy directly from the Web, or download the data and print it later. Text usually prints quickly. Images may take a long time, so if they are not necessary, remove them before printing.

To save a web page you are at, from the **File** menu, select **Save As**. The **Save As** dialogue box will be displayed. Select the location where you want to save the data. A filename is suggested, but you can change it if you wish.

Figure 8.14 Saving as a web page

In the **Save as type** section, select **Web Page, complete** from the list. Click on **Save**.

▭ GIVE IT A GO   saving a web page

Go to the Heinemann website and save the home page onto your computer.

• • • *Exporting to other applications*

If you want to take text and/or images from a web page and change them or use them for your own purposes in another document, the quickest way is to *export* the information into another application.

To do this, highlight either the text or graphic that you wish to save. Once your selection is made, select **Copy** from the **Edit** menu, go to the application (such as Publisher or Word) into which you wish to save the objects and paste into that application.

If you wish to copy the whole file choose **Select All** from the **Edit** menu.

■■■ EVIDENCE ACTIVITY

Exporting to another application

1   Go to the Heinemann website and select the Heinemann logo.

2   Export the logo into a new Word document.

3   Type into the new document:

> This is the Heinemann logo, exported by [your name] from the Heinemann website.

4   Save and print the document.

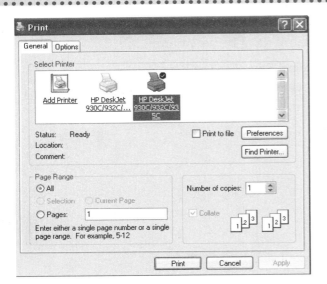

••• *Printing*

To print a web page directly from your web browser, select **Print** from the **File** menu, or click on the **Print** icon. When the Print dialogue box is displayed make your selections, then click on **OK**.

Note that if the web page is divided into frames, enter your choices in the **Print Frames** section, on the **Options** tab.

Figure 8.15 The Print dialogue box

■■■ EVIDENCE ACTIVITIES

A user guide to the Internet

Produce a user guide outlining responsible use of the Internet.

Describe in your guide how to set up an account. You can use the summary you wrote in the *Setting up on the Internet: user-guide* activity on page 128.

You may download useful data or images into your work. See Unit 7 for information on the production of a user guide.

The effect of the Internet on our lives

1   List the effects that you think the Internet has had on our lives.

2   Overall, do you think the effects have been good or bad?

3   Give two examples of how using the Internet has had a good effect on our lives.

4   Give two examples of how using the Internet has had a bad effect on our lives.

unit 9

IT applications

This unit has been designed to allow you to learn how to use IT applications. You will use them to produce documents, spreadsheets, and a presentation. You will find out about layout, how to use images, charts and graphs.

When you are preparing any work it is important to consider who it is for — who is going to be looking at it, using it, or listening to it. You have to know your audience — this will affect the way in which you present the material. This is true whether it is a business letter, accounts on a spreadsheet or a presentation of a new product.

All the applications can be used together, and materials produced in one can be imported and used in any of the others. You are going to prepare work using a word processing application, and use it in the presentation application. When you carry out the case study you should think about how you will prepare and present the information and, importantly, consider your audience.

In this unit you will need to learn about:

▷ word processing software

▷ spreadsheet software

▷ how to use software to create a presentation

▷ how to create and use graphical images.

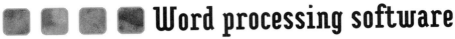

Word processing software

This software allows you to enter or import text and images. You can alter, amend and format the text in many ways. The software also allows you to check your spelling and grammar.

It is the most widely used software in business and in the home. It is easy to produce professional-looking documents. They can be saved and recalled, altered and printed. You can produce business documents. There is a range of templates you can use including those for faxes, email messages, web pages, publications such as brochures and manuals, memos, and agendas. There are also a number of wizards, which are guides to take you through the creation of documents. Most of the templates have a wizard – there is even one for creating your CV.

Microsoft Word is the word processing program we will be using in this section. You will create a business letter, a memo, a brochure including a table, and a menu.

Parts of the document window

The first thing you see when you have loaded Word the document window. Figure 9.1 shows a blank document, with default values (the pre-programmed settings such as margins, font type and size, line spacing and alignment). The settings will remain unchanged until you alter them.

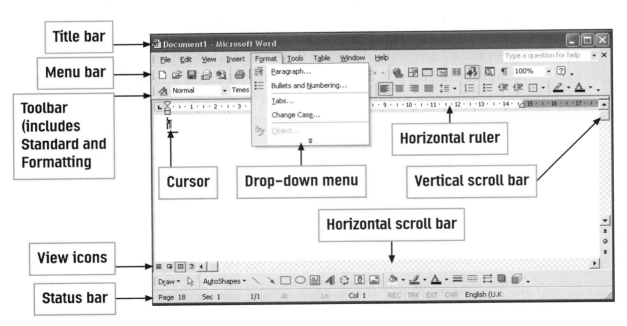

Figure 9.1 The Word document window

FEATURE	FUNCTION
Cursor	This shows your position on the screen and where your next text will appear.
Horizontal ruler	This shows the position of text and can be displayed in centimetres or inches.
Scroll bars	These allow you to move quickly through the document.
Status bar	This provides information about the page you are currently working on, the position of the cursor and the text on your screen.
View icons	There are different ways of viewing your text – Normal, Print Layout, Outline View and Web Layout View.
Title bar	This shows the name of the application being used (Microsoft Word) and the current document name, in this case, Document1 (the default).
Menu bar	This has menu names, which can be selected using the mouse or via the keyboard. When selected, a drop-down menu displays further options. Initially it displays the options used most recently. After a few seconds, the drop-down menu expands to include all available options.
Standard toolbar	This contains shortcut icons to select actions that are used frequently. For example, to open a new file, click on the button shown in Figure 9.2.
Formatting toolbar	This contains formatting shortcuts such as underlining and centring text: see Figure 9.3.

GIVE IT A GO · getting started with Word

Load Word, and begin to familiarise yourself with all the functions in a document window.

Remember that your system may be different from the one used in this example, and different buttons may be displayed. To find out what each button on your toolbar does, point the mouse over the button and wait a few seconds. A box will appear giving a brief explanation of the button – this is known as a *ToolTip*.

Text can be formatted or enhanced in a number of ways – you can add bullet and number points, emboldening, italics or underling and change the alignment. Make a note of how to carry out these actions as you will be using them in following activities.

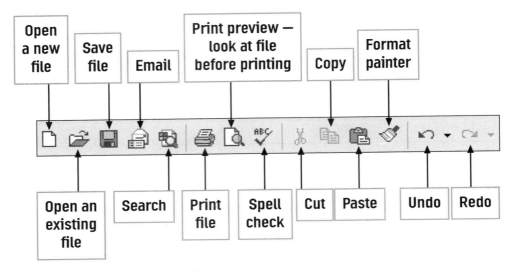

Figure 9.2 Standard toolbar buttons

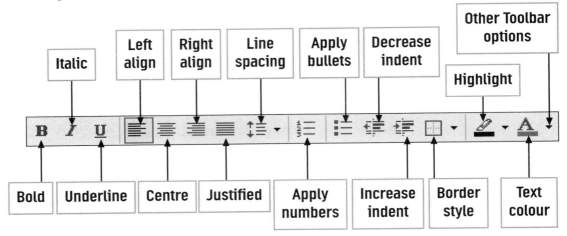

Figure 9.3 Formatting toolbar buttons

Different types of document

There are a number of different types of document. They include business letters, memoranda (memos) and reports. Business letters are written in a more formal style than personal letters. A memo is an internal note within a company and is often less formal than a letter. A report is usually a longer document, written in a formal style, and is generally on a specified subject. When writing any of these documents it is important to remember who they are being sent to, and you should use the appropriate style and language.

Formatting and layout

When you have entered text it is possible to edit (change) your work, and also to format it and alter the way it is presented. You may find the Format painter useful – it allows you to copy the format of text you choose to any other text. If you click on the relevant icon (the brush, Standard toolbar) and then 'brush' selected text, it will change the format of the text to the format of where the cursor was previously.

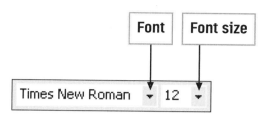

Figure 9.4 Toolbar options – font and font size

• • • *Font and font size*

To change the font or the font size, click on the down arrow at the end of the font name box on the Formatting toolbar and make your selection. Remember to select a style that is suitable for the purpose. A more decorative font is suitable for bulletins, brochures and menus.

• • • *Margins and orientation*

You can alter the margins – the blank space at the sides, top and bottom of the page. To do so, select **Page Setup** from the **File** menu. The **Page Setup** dialogue box will be displayed.

You can change the way the text appears on the page (i.e. its orientation) to be portrait or landscape.

Portrait orientation means the shorter side to the top.

Landscape orientation means the longer side to the top.

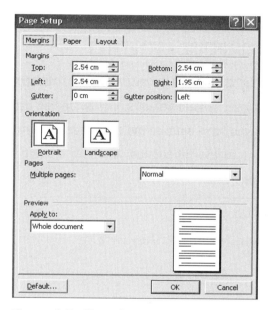

Figure 9.5 Changing margins and orientation

• • • *Headers and footers*

Headers and footers are text that can be made to appear automatically at the top or bottom of each page in a document. To set them up, select **Header and Footer** from the **View** menu. You can then enter any text that you require. You can use the shortcut buttons.

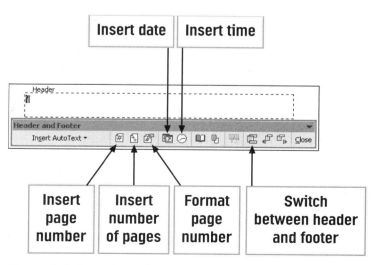

Figure 9.6 Inserting a header

Alternatively, you can use the down arrow at the end of the **Insert AutoText** box and select from the options given.

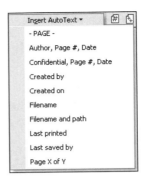

Figure 9.7 **Using options from the Insert AutoText menu**

▦▦▦ EVIDENCE ACTIVITIES

Creating a word-processed document

1   Using your system defaults, key in the text below. The line endings will be different in your work.

2   When you have entered the text, check it carefully (including using the spell checker).

3   Check that it is left aligned, and save it using the filename **U9DIAM**.

4   Print one copy.

DIAMONDS

Each stone is unique. They vary in:

Colour
Cut
Clarity
Size.

Diamonds vary in colour from brilliant white or blue white to black. The more colourless a diamond, the rarer and more expensive it is. The exception to this rule is a stone which has naturally bright colours, such as the Hope Blue or Dresden Green.

It is extremely rare to find a diamond without minor imperfections (known as inclusions). Such imperfections may not even be visible to the naked eye. Fewer inclusions give greater clarity and brilliance and increase the value.

The brilliance of a stone is drawn out by the cutter. Various cuts are used, the most common being the brilliant cut.

Caratage is the weight of a diamond, which is also an indication of its size, and is used in conjunction with colour, clarity and cut to determine the value of the diamond.

Formatting a word-processed document

1   Load the work saved at the end of the previous activity, file name U9EX1.

2   Underline and centre the heading DIAMONDS.

3   Embolden and add bullet points to the text: Colour Cut Clarity Size.

4   Set the text *Hope Blue* and *Dresden Green* in italics.

5   Set all the margins to 3 cm.

6   Add a footer from the Insert AutoText menu — Author, Page #, Date.

7   Change the alignment of the entire file to fully justified.

8   Use Arial font, size 12.

9   Save your work using the filename **U9DIAM2**, and print one copy.

• • • *Using templates*

Word provides a number of templates for your use. To open a template, select **New** from the **File** menu. The **New Document** pane will be displayed on your screen. Under **New from template** select **General Templates**. Under the **Letters and Faxes** tab, select **Professional Letter**, then click on **OK**.

A new document will be set up. Follow the instructions on screen and enter your text.

■■■ EVIDENCE ACTIVITY

Using templates

1   Key in the letter below using the Professional Letter template. Choose a company name, and enter your own details where it specifies: [Click here and type return address].

2   Make sure the date is entered correctly.

3   Send the letter to: Miss Linda Clark, 230 High Street, Pontefract, PN3 7JJ

4   Use this text for the body of the letter:

> Thank you for your letter regarding your recent purchase of one of our products. I am sorry that you are experiencing difficulty.
>
> I have arranged for an engineer to visit your premises on Thursday of next week, at 14:00 hours. If this is not convenient, perhaps you could telephone and arrange an alternative appointment.

5   Enter your own name where it says [Click here and type your name].

6   Save your work using the filename **U9TEMPL**, and print one copy.

• • • *Using tables*

To present data in a table, select **Insert**, then **Table** from the **Table** menu. The **Insert Table** dialogue box will be displayed.

Under table size enter the dimensions of the table you want to create, then click on **OK**.

Figure 9.8 Using the Table function

■■■ EVIDENCE ACTIVITY

Using tables

Create a leaflet using the text below, including the table, making sure that it will fit onto A5 paper (14.8 cm×21 cm). Centre the text on the page. You can select the fonts and font sizes, and any enhancements and colours. Save your work using the filename **U9TABLES**, and print one copy.

COMPUTERS-4-U
345 NEWSOME ROAD
WALTON

0151 600 1290

WHILE STOCK LASTS
END OF LINE SALE

MODEL	PRICE	NO IN STOCK	DISCOUNT
GBR564	£1250.99	8	25%
FRE209	£1585.00	15	35%
DHE401	£1355.75	25	50%

OPENING HOURS

MONDAY TO SATURDAY
08:30 – 20:00

• • • *House style*

Many companies specify how work should be prepared so that they present a consistent image. This is known as the house style. It may include a header or footer, but will always specify the font and font sizes to be used. Other items that may be included are shown in the example below.

Text style

FEATURE	FONT	POINT SIZE	STYLE	ALIGNMENT	
Heading	Arial	16	Bold	Centred	
Sub Heading	Arial	12	Italic	Left	
Body	Arial	11		Justified	
Bullet text	Arial	10	Italic	Left	
Table	Arial	10	Bold	Centre	Column heading
				Left	Row heading
				Left	Text

Reports

Header	Arial	10	Regular	Left	automatic date field
Footer	Arial	10	Regular	Left	name of author
				Centre	file name
				Right	automatic page no
Line spacing			Double		

• • • *Pagination*

When you have done a lot of formatting, or re-formatting, you should check where the text ends on each page. You can control where automatic page breaks are placed by setting pagination options. You can do this by selecting **Paragraph** from the **Format** menu, then going to the **Line and Page Breaks** tab. Your options are:

- keep lines of a paragraph together on a page or in a column
- keep paragraphs together on a page
- always force a page break before a paragraph
- control widow and orphan lines (this option is turned **on** by default)

▣▣▣ EVIDENCE ACTIVITY

Using house style

Load the file named **U9report** — your tutor will tell you where to find it. Re-format the report using the house style above. Save your work using the filename **U9STYLE**, and print one copy.

Version management

• • • Saving versions of documents

To record changes made to a file, you can save multiple versions within the same file. This saves disk space because the program saves only the differences between versions, not an entire copy of each version. You can go back and review, open, print, and delete earlier versions. A record is made of who made the changes and when.

There are two ways of saving a version of a document:

- *Manually*: You can save a version in its current state at any time, i.e. you might save the version, send it for review (that is, others insert revision marks and comments), and after including review changes, save another version. To do this select **Versions** from the **File** menu, and then press **Save Now**. You then have the opportunity to record any comments before clicking **OK**.
- *Automatically*: Word can automatically save a version each time the document is saved and closed. To do this you select **Versions** from the **File** menu, and then click **the Automatically save a version on close** check box, before clicking **Close**.

To view a version you have saved, you only need to return to the **Versions** box, and select one of the existing versions listed and then click on **Open**.

• • • Save a version as a separate file

If you have multiple versions in one file, there are three instances when you may want to save one version as a separate file:

- if you want to modify a version of a document (because document versions are archived, they can otherwise only be viewed, printed or deleted)
- if the file contains several versions, and you want to make sure that only the most recent version is reviewed – this will prevent anyone from opening earlier versions
- if you want to compare an earlier version with the current version of the document. (Once you have saved the version separately, the way to make this comparison is to choose **Track Changes** from the **Tools** menu, and then choose **Compare Documents**.)

To save a version as a separate file, open the version you want to save separately, as normal, then select **Save As** from the **File** menu, and follow the instructions under 'Saving a file as a Word document' below. Note that you cannot use versioning to save a document as a web page.

● ● ● *Other recovery facilities*

Saving versions of a document is different from saving a backup copy. A backup is to ensure against data loss or unintended changes. When backup saving is turned on, a new backup replaces the existing backup each time the file is saved.

Backup saving is turned on by selecting **Options** from the **Tools** menu, then selecting **Save**, and the **Always create backup copy** check box. Note that there is also a check box for **AutoRecover**. This facility means Word automatically saves a temporary copy of your document as often as you choose – but this is deleted whenever you save or close the document. It is of most use in the event that Word 'freezes' or the computer 'crashes' before you have saved your document.

File management

● ● ● *Saving a file as a Word document*

Select **Save As** from the **File** menu. The Save As dialogue box will be displayed. At the bottom of the window you will see the **Save as type** box.

When you click on the down arrow at the end of this box a drop-down menu is displayed. You can select the type of document you want to create.

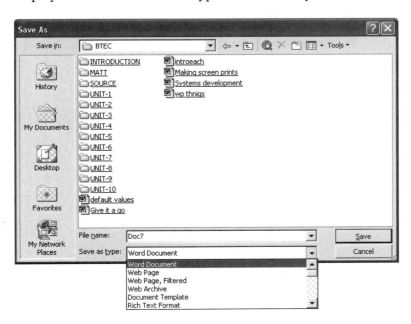

Figure 9.9 The Save As dialogue box

● ● ● *Printing*

To print a file, select **Print** from the **File** menu. The **Print** dialogue box will be displayed.

Under **Page range** you can choose to print the entire file, the current page, or specified pages.

Click on **OK**.

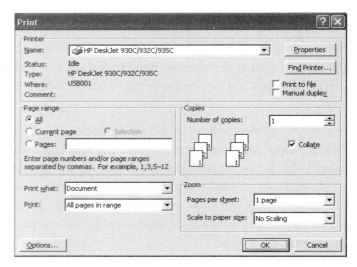

Figure 9.10 The Print dialogue box

● ● ● *Creating a new folder*

Folders are a method of keeping all documents with the same theme together. Sub folders are, in effect, just other folders in a main folder. See Unit 3 for further details.

To create a new folder, go to the location where you want to create the folder (or sub folder). In this case, we start in the folder **My Documents**.

Under **File and Folder Tasks**, select **Make a new folder**.

A folder will be created with the file name **New Folder**. Replace this with the file name you require.

Alternatively, you can select **New**, then **Folder** from the **File** menu.

Figure 9.11 Creating a new folder

Spreadsheet software

Purpose

This software is used to produce work using figures, such as:

- personal budgets (an account of money earned and money spent)
- petty cash records (a record of small amounts of money held in a company for minor expenses such as stationery)
- profit and loss accounts (an account of money earned by a company and the money spent).

You can enter text and figures and use formulae to add, subtract, divide and multiply the figures. There are automatic functions that allow you to calculate the sum and average of a series of figures. You can alter and amend the data. You can format it in much the same way as you do in Word. There is a spellcheck facility.

One of the most useful facilities is the ability to display the figures as a chart or graph. There is a chart wizard to help you to develop the chart of your choice (such as pie or bar charts). There are a number of templates and wizards for more advanced work.

A spreadsheet consists of a large grid into which you enter text and data. When changes are made the spreadsheet automatically recalculates new values. You can also use it as a database or a filing system – data can be sorted and searched. It is very fast, accurate and is used widely in business and in the home.

Microsoft Excel is a spreadsheet program. In this section we will be using it to work with a number of worksheets including a personal budget, a sales forecasting summary, and survey results.

Entering and manipulating data

● ● ● *Parts of the workbook window*

When you load Microsoft Excel, the Excel window is displayed, showing a blank sheet and the New Workbook pane on the right of the screen.

You will see that the shortcut icons on the toolbars are similar to those in Word, but there are also icons specifically used by Excel. These include those identified on Figures 9.12 and 9.13.

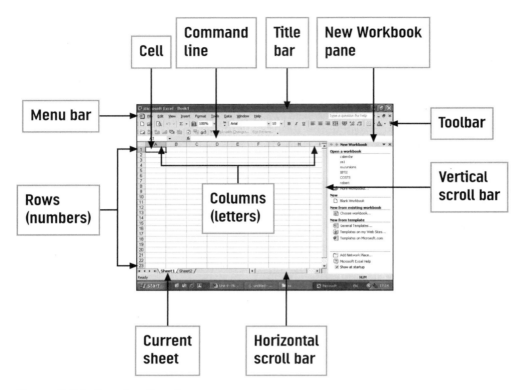

Figure 9.12 Opening Excel

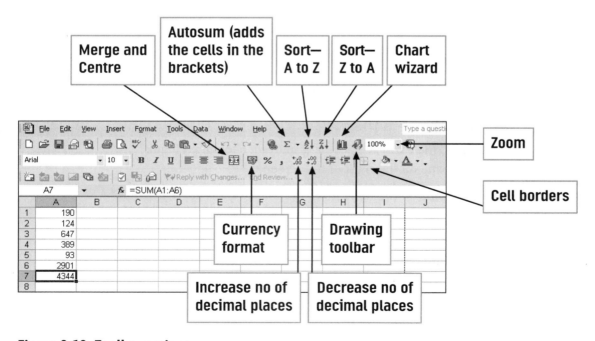

Figure 9.13 Toolbar options

• • • *Spreadsheet structure*

As you can see from the Figures, a spreadsheet is structured in the following way:

- *Row*: This is a line of cells across the spreadsheet. Each row has a reference number.
- *Column*: This is a line of cells down the spreadsheet. Each column has a reference letter.
- *Cell*: A single 'box' on the spreadsheet grid is called a cell.
- *Cell references*: Each cell can be identified by giving its row and column reference, like map referencing. If you click on a cell, the reference is shown to the left of the Command line. Cell references are essential to the writing of formulae, which are how you make calculations on a spreadsheet.

GIVE IT A GO | inputting spreadsheet data

Load Microsoft Excel and take some time to familiarise yourself with the layout and icons.

1   As shown in Figure 9.13, in cells A1 to A6 enter: 190, 124, 647, 389, 93, 2901. You should always enter numeric data **very carefully**. Incorrect entries will make the results inaccurate.

2   Go to cell A7. Click on the **AutoSum** button. Dotted lines will show what cells the function is automatically adding up. Both the cell and the Command line will show the formula that AutoSum is using. Press Return on your keyboard. The result will be placed in cell A7.

• • • *Formatting cells*

Apart from the usual formatting of text, there are formatting options in Excel specific to spreadsheets. You can specify an individual cell or a range of cells (a row, column or selection you make) to make these changes. These can be accessed by using the shortcut icons on the Toolbar. They include:

- *Text*: You can specify the layout of text within cells – it can be displayed left aligned, right aligned or centred. The Merge and Centre button joins selected cells together and centres the text between them – useful for overall table headings. Note that it is more common to align numbers to the *right*.
- *Numeric data*: You can choose to display in pounds and pence, as a percentage, or with different decimal places. This last option means you can display data in integer format (i.e. to the nearest whole number).
- *Graphics*: You can put borders around cells or groups of cells, fill them with shades of colour, or colour the text.

• • • *Editing data*

Once you have added any sort of data to a cell, it can be changed or deleted.

To edit the contents of a cell, double-click on the cell and make the change. If it has a hidden formula, that is what you will see – and the other cells that the formula effects will also be highlighted. You can then edit the formula. To delete the contents of a cell, just click on it and press the keyboard delete button, or just start typing.

To edit whole cells; highlight individual cells or a whole row or column, and either insert new cells using the **Insert** menu, or **Delete** them under the **Edit** menu – you will be asked what adjustments you want as a result of the deletion.

• • • *Moving or copying data*

There are many ways of moving or copying data in Excel. Select the cell (or cell range), then:

- *Move entire cell (formulas, formats etc.)*: Point to the border of the cell until your pointer turns into an arrow; click and drag to the new position; or **Cut** and **Paste** using the shortcut icons, or via the **Edit** menu.
- *Copy entire cell to a separate location*: Do the same as above, except hold down **Alt** while you drag, then release at the destination cell; or **Copy** and **Paste** using the shortcut icons, or via the **Edit** menu.
- *Copy entire cell to adjacent location*: Point to the bottom right-hand corner of the cell until your pointer turns into a black cross, then click and drag. The spreadsheet will automatically 'advance' the formula.
- *Copy only formats of a cell*: Click the **Format Painter** icon (the brush) then select where you want to copy the format to.
- *Copy only aspects of a cell (e.g. formulas only)*: Click the Copy icon or choose **Copy** from the **Edit** menu, then select the upper-left cell of the area you want to paste into. Then choose **Paste Special** from the **Edit** menu, choose one of the options in the dialogue box, then click **OK**.

• • • *Sorting data*

You can sort data in your spreadsheet. You may want to do this if you have additional data – enter it below the current data and then sort it into the order you prefer. You may want to reorganise your data into different groupings; view it in order of the amount, or in alphabetical order. When you sort it is essential that you include any associated data.

In Figure 9.14 you can see that the data to be sorted is highlighted – the labels and figures for Sales and Property.

Once the data is highlighted, click on the **Sort Ascending** (A-Z) button on the toolbar. The **Sort** dialogue box is displayed. The sort in this case will be carried out on Column A.

You can carry out up to three sorts on the data, each of which can be ascending or descending.

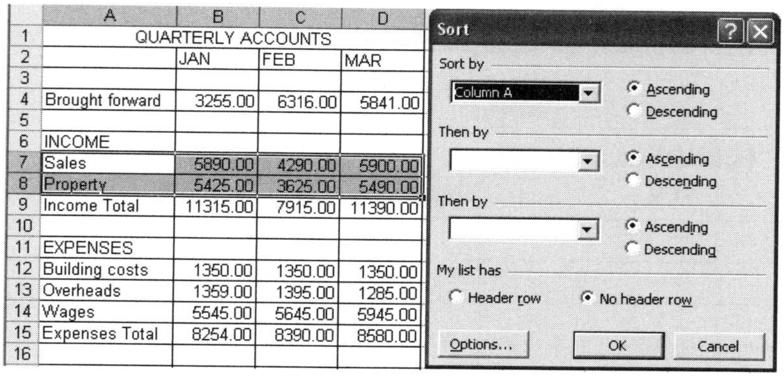

Figure 9.14 Sorting data

Formulae

Formulae are the key to how spreadsheets make calculations and present data. They are the sums or equations that you type into a cell, which draws information from other cells to give an answer. Formulae use cell references to bring numbers together. For example, '=A1+A6' means to add together the numbers in those two cells.

● ● ● *Entering a formula*

To enter a formula, you click on a cell, and then type '=' into it, and start writing the formula – or you write it into the Command line. You can click on other cells or ranges of cells while doing the formula, and the cell references will automatically come up. This can save time.

When entering formulae you use:

+   for addition
-   for subtraction
*   for multiplication
/   for division.

● ● ● *Functions*

These are instructions to carry out a process. Each function has a word that the program recognises. For example, SUM(A1:D20) will add all the numbers stored in the cells from A1 down to and including D20.

As you have already experienced, the SUM function has a shortcut icon because it is the most used function. There are other functions, under the Function icon on the Command line.

■■■ EVIDENCE ACTIVITY

Preparing a spreadsheet

1 You are going to enter your personal budget onto a spreadsheet. Enter the framework shown below. Check the spelling on your work.

PERSONAL BUDGET				
	JAN	FEB	MAR	TOTAL
INCOME				
Wages				
Tips				
Bonuses				
Income Total				
EXPENSES				
Rent				
Council Tax				
Gas and Electricity				
Food				
Fares				
Leisure				
Expenses Total				
REMAINING				

2 Enter your own data into the spreadsheet. (Note: if you are doing Unit 6, you will already have collected this information.)

3 Using the relevant formula, calculate the Income Total for JAN. Replicate the formula for FEB and MAR.

4 Using the relevant formula, calculate the Expenses Total for JAN. Replicate the formula for FEB and MAR.

5 Using the relevant formula, calculate the figure REMAINING (Income Total minus Expenses Total) for JAN. Replicate the formula for FEB and MAR.

6 In the TOTAL column, using the relevant formula, calculate the TOTAL Wages for JAN, FEB and MAR. Replicate the formula for all the other items. Make sure you do not replicate the formula into a row where there is no data.

7 Using the Merge and Centre button, centre the title over all the columns.

8 Place borders around all the cells.

9 Save your work using the file name **U9SS1**.

10 Print a copy of your work.

Converting data to a suitable graph or chart

You can use Excel to create a large number of different charts and graphs. The most common, and the charts you will be using, are pie charts and bar or column charts:

- *Pie chart*: This uses one set of data and shows the portion for each item of data.
- *Bar chart*: This uses one or more sets of data and compares the relative values.
- *Column chart*: This uses one or more sets of data and compares the relative values.

There is some confusion between bar and column charts. Many think of a bar chart in the way that Excel displays a column chart. The difference is in the way the data is displayed – either top to bottom (column) or left to right (bar).

You can enter data, and then, using the chart wizard, convert that data into a suitable chart or graph.

• • • *Using the chart wizard*

In order to create a chart, first the data must be highlighted.

On the toolbar, click on the **Chart Wizard** icon. The Chart Wizard dialogue box will be displayed showing the first screen of four: **Step 1 of 4 – Chart Type**. The chart type that is selected (the default) is **Column**.

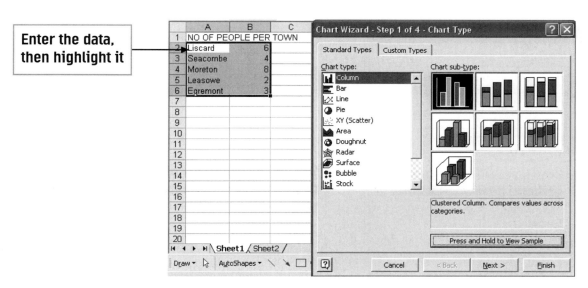

Figure 9.15 Using the Chart Wizard – Step 1 of 4

At this point, if you use the button on the wizard **Press and Hold to View Sample**, the highlighted data will be displayed in the chosen **Chart type** – this means you can try several types before settling on one.

When you have finished, click on **Next**.

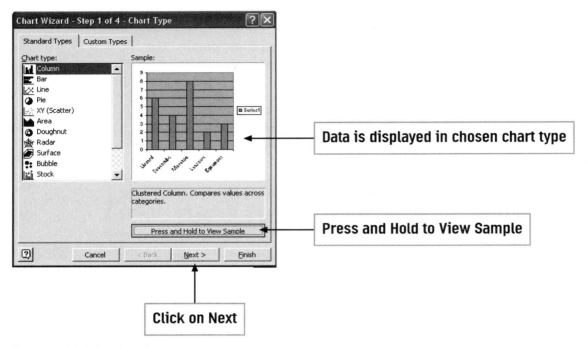

Figure 9.16 Viewing the data

Step 2 of 4 – Chart Source Data is displayed.

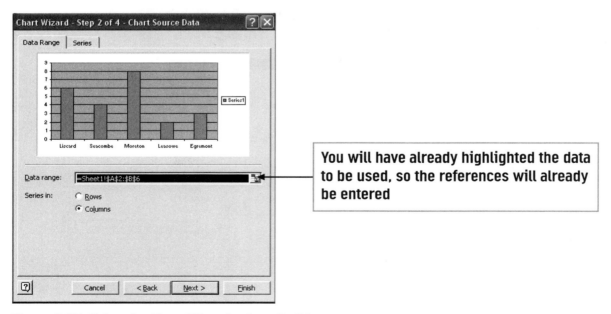

Figure 9.17 Using the Chart Wizard – Step 2 of 4

Clicking on **Next** will take you to **Step 3 of 4 – Chart Options**, with the **Titles** tab displayed.

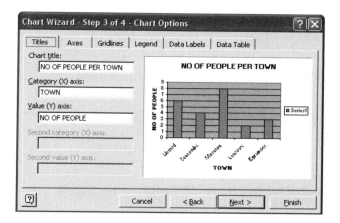

Figure 9.18 Using the Chart Wizard – Step 3 of 4

This is where you enter your chart title, and headings for the X and Y axis.

The rest of the tabs offer other design options you can choose from for looks or purpose reasons. Every action is easy to reverse, so it is worth experimenting.

The final step, **Step 3 of 4 – Chart Location**, offers saving options for the chart. You can save it on the spreadsheet **OR** as a new sheet with a new name. (New sheets can be viewed at the bottom of the screen, where it is possible to switch between sheets by clicking on the tabs.)

Finally, you click **Finish**.

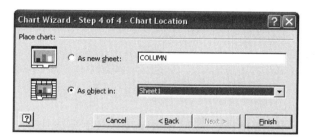

Figure 9.19 Using the Chart Wizard – Step 4 of 4

Pie charts

When you are creating a pie chart you can display either the values or the percentage – or you can even click both.

Click the **Value** box to display numbers.

Click the **Percentage** box to display percentages.

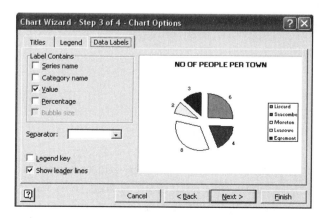

Figure 9.20 Displaying values

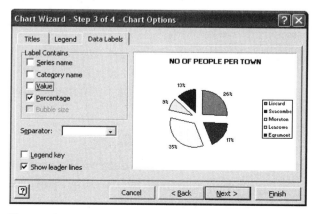

Figure 9.21 Displaying percentages

■■■ EVIDENCE ACTIVITY

Using the chart wizard

You are going to create a column chart, using the chart wizard, showing the number of people who live in each town or district.

1 Carry out a survey in your group to identify the area in which people live. Keep it very simple, just use the town or district.

2 Count the number of people who live in *each* town or district.

3 Enter the results into a spreadsheet, making sure that the figures are in integer format (as in Figure 9.15).

4 Produce a column chart from the data.

5 Use the title NO OF PEOPLE PER TOWN.

6 Display the legend.

7 Save your work using the file name **U9SSGRAPHS**.

● ● ● *Other facilities*

You can add a header or footer to your work in the same way as you did in Word (see page 147). You can also change the orientation. To carry out these tasks select **Page Setup** from the **File** menu. The **Page Setup** dialogue box is displayed.

Change the orientation here

Figure 9.22 The Page Setup dialogue box

GIVE IT A GO page setup

Try the other tabs to see the options that you have on each of them.

Printing

To print the data or any of the charts you have created, follow the same method as for Word, by selecting **Print** from the **File** menu. You have more options than for Word: for example you can print the whole spreadsheet or only part of it, and this can be done in three ways: the figures; the formulae; as a chart or graph.

Using software to create a presentation

A presentation graphics program allows you to set up slides and slide shows incorporating prepared text and images to make your presentations more dynamic and interesting. In this section we will be using Microsoft PowerPoint.

Suitability for specified audience

When preparing a presentation you must consider who it is aimed at and use suitable and appropriate text and images to interest that group. For example, to sell a new product you would probably want to outline the product specification, the value of the item, the advantages the product has over a similar product produced by competitors, etc. You would probably incorporate images of the product itself.

If you were trying to attract potential business customers you would probably want to include the advantages to their company of selecting your product or service. On the other hand, if the presentation was for your own work colleagues you would probably adopt a more informal approach.

Tools

The main features of the program include:

FEATURE	FUNCTION
Design templates	These contain colour schemes and custom formatting that will be applied to any slides you create.
Wizards	These are automated procedures that guide you through tasks.
Creating a slide style	This is carried out on a 'master' slide and then applied to any other slide you create in that presentation. It can include text and graphics.
Graphic size and position	You can increase or decrease the size of any graphic you import, and move the graphic to any position on the slide.
Select background colour	You can select the colour, pattern or image onto which you place your slide material.
Formatting	You can select the font and font size. You can also apply bullets, select alignment (left, centre and right), choose the text colour and enhance it (bold, underline or italics).
Transitions and animations	These set up features in your presentation including how the slides appear on the screen, and how you move to the next slide.
Timings	You can set up the length of time your slides remain on screen.

• • • *Parts of the presentation window*

When you load Microsoft PowerPoint, the PowerPoint window is displayed, showing a blank presentation, and the New Presentation pane on the right of the screen.

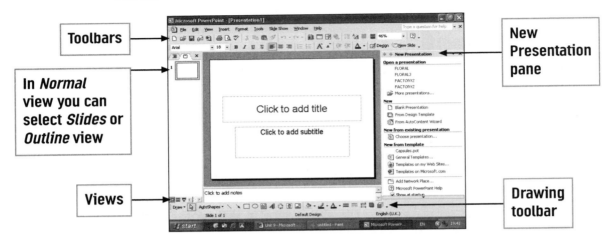

Figure 9.23 PowerPoint opening window

• • • *Setting up a master slide*

Before you start putting text or images onto your slides, it is always best to save the slide layout and design as a master slide. In doing so, you create the way you want the file to look and any further slides you create will have the same features – this will save you time as well as create a consistent look.

To set up a master slide, select **Master, Slide Master** from the **View** menu. In the top box, click on **Click to edit the Master title style**, and using the buttons on the toolbar, choose formatting options for the text. Similarly, click on **Click to edit Master text style** to choose options for the main text, and for any further levels of text you may need (delete those you don't need).

• • • *Entering text or images into a slide*

You can enter or import text and image files into a master slide, as with other slides, but remember that this will be repeated on all your slides.

When you have set up the master page, you can return to the default first blank presentation slide by selecting **Normal** from the **View** menu. Alternatively, you can click on the left-hand Views shortcut icon.

To enter text, type into the **Click to add title** and **Click to add subtitle** boxes. To add an image, select **Picture, From File** from the **Insert** menu. Note that **Movies and Sounds** can also be imported from this menu. To import text from Word, you can either copy and paste from the Word document, or: in Word, select **Send To** from the **File** menu, then select **Microsoft Powerpoint**.

■■■ EVIDENCE ACTIVITY

Creating a presentation

You are going to create a presentation called DIAMONDS, using material your tutor will give you.

1   First, set up a Master Slide. Use the following formatting:
   - Master Title: Tahoma font, size 40, bold, centered, dark red
   - Master Text: Tahoma font, size 36, normal, left aligned, black
   - Master Text second level: Tahoma font, size 32, italic, left aligned, black.

2   Insert the image **DIAMOND** (ask your tutor for the location of the file) into the **Master Slide**. Place the image in the bottom right hand corner of the slide. It should be roughly 4 cm by 4 cm.

3   In **Normal** view, enter DIAMONDS into the title box, and your name and today's date into the subtitle box (choose **Date and Time** formats from the **Insert** menu).

4   To save your work, select **Save As** from the **File** menu, choose a location and use the file name **DIAMOND1**.

● ● ● *Managing slides*

To add a new slide
Click on the **New Slide** button on the toolbar. The **Slide Layout** pane is displayed. There are various AutoLayouts you can choose for the new slide. The **Title and Text** layout will match the default layout that you may have started with. This slide layout has a page-wide title frame at the top of the page, and a page-wide frame below the title frame. (If you want to change the layout of an existing slide, go direct to the **Slide Layout** icon on the toolbar.)

To insert slide numbers
Click on **View, Master, Slide Master**. Select **View, Header and Footer**, click on **Slide number** then on **Apply to All**.

To change the order of slides
Select **Slide Sorter** from the **View** menu (or go to the Views shortcut icons). Click on the slide you want to move. Drag and place the slide in the new position.

To delete a slide
Go to the slide you want to remove, and click on **Edit, Delete Slide**. Another way is to go to **Slide Sorter**, select the slide and delete it using the keyboard delete.

■■■ EVIDENCE ACTIVITY

Managing slides

1 Open **DIAMOND1**. Create a new slide.

2 Complete slide 2 by using the file **DIAMONDS** which your tutor will give you. Create and complete new slides using DIAMONDS until you have six slides.

3 Insert slide numbers using the **Slide Master**.

4 Change the order of the slides, so that slide 6, '**What do you look for?**' becomes slide 2.

5 Delete slide 6, now called '**Size**'.

6 On the toolbar, click on the spelling button to check your work.

7 Insert slide numbers using the **Slide Master**.

8 Save your work.

••• *Applying transitions and timings*

When you start a slide show, normally each click of the mouse brings up a new slide. However, you can also bring up the parts of the slide separately and in different ways.

In this version of Office the manner in which the animations are constructed varies – some have a built-in transition and some do not. They are also split into three groups, **Subtle**, **Moderate** and **Exciting**.

To apply an animation

1) From the **View** menu select **Slide Sorter**.
2) Select at least one of the slides, and on the toolbar, click on the **Design** icon. The **Slide Design** pane is displayed.
3) Select **Animation Schemes** and a list will be displayed.
4) Make your selection to apply to a slide, or click on **Apply to All Slides**.
5) An **Animation Schemes** icon will be displayed below each of the slides.
6) Close the **Slide Design** frame.

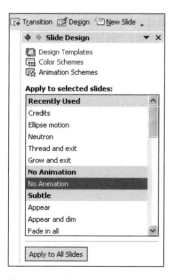

Figure 9.24 Applying animations

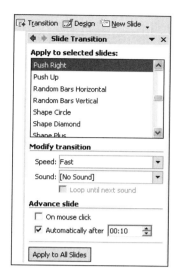

Figure 9.25 Applying timings

To apply timings

1) Select **Slide Sorter** from the **View** menu.
2) Select at least one of the slides, and on the toolbar, click on the **Transition** icon. The **Slide Transition** pane is displayed.
3) As well as applying transition styles, there are options to modify the transition and also as to whether the slides move on automatically or not. In Figure 9.26, the slides have been set to advance **Automatically after** 10 seconds.
4) To apply the timing to **all** the slides, click on **Apply to All Slides**.
5) Close the **Slide Transition** pane.

••• *Running a slide show*

To run your slide show, select **View Show** from the **Slide Show** menu, or the **View Show** icon, which is grouped with the View icons.

The first slide will fill the screen, and clicks of the mouse will bring on the next slide – or the next animation, whatever you have set up. If you need to interrupt the show at any time, press the keyboard escape button. Viewing your show and practicing your presentation with it, is the best way of checking that you have got the animations and timings right.

▢▢▢ EVIDENCE ACTIVITY

Transitions and timings

You are going to add transitions and timings to your presentation.

1   Open your presentation **DIAMOND1**.

2   Apply the animation of your choice to all the slides in the presentation.

3   Apply an automatic timing of 12 seconds to all the slides in the presentation.

4   Save your work using the same file name, and close the presentation.

••• *Printing*

You can print your presentation in a number of ways.

First, open your presentation. From the **File** menu, select **Print**. When the **Print** dialogue box is displayed, select how you want to print the presentation under **Print what**.

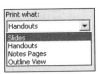

Figure 9.26 Print options

You are presented with several options. This is what they mean:

Figure 9.27 Layout for 3 slides per page

- *Slides*: This means print a copy of all or individual slides, with full formatting.
- *Outline View*: This means print a copy of the text on the slides.

Figure 9.28 Layout for 6 slides per page

- *Notes Pages*: This means print the slides with a copy of the speaker's notes on. Notes are attached to the slides to help the speaker make specific points. They are not actually shown in a slideshow; only the speaker can see them on a print out. There is a **Click to add notes** area at the bottom of each slide screen.
- *Audience handouts*: This means print a 'reduced' copy of the slides with space for the audience to make their own notes. The layout varies depending on how many slides are printed on each page. If you select **Handouts**, you can make further choices on the number of slides displayed on each page. You can select 1, 2, 3, 4, 6, or 9. The layout varies depending on the number you choose – you can see the layout for three slides per page and six slides per page below.

Printing individual slides

There is also the option within the **Print dialogue** box to choose the **Print** range – if you select this, you can select **Current slide** to print an individual slide, or **All** to print all of them.

GIVE IT A GO print a presentation

You are going to print your presentation in different formats.

1 Open your presentation **DIAMOND1**.

2 Print your presentation in **Outline View**.

3 Print your presentation as **Handouts** – three per page.

4 Print a copy of slide 1 and slide 4.

5 Close your presentation.

Creating and using graphical images

There is a range of sources from which you can get images that you want to use in your work. You can import images from clip art, download them from the Internet, produce them on a digital camera, scan them using a scanner, or create them yourself using a computer art program.

Images are used to enhance work. They can be used in many applications including word processing, desktop publishing, presentation graphics and web pages. You will have seen them being used to illustrate:

- destinations in holiday brochures
- products in a catalogue
- the property in estate agents' house details.

Art programs

A computer art program allows you to design and draw your own designs, as well as import images from clip art, images downloaded from the Internet, or photographs from a digital camera, and to alter them to meet your requirements.

You will be provided with a brush facility, to allow you to draw freely. You can add text in a variety of styles, fonts and sizes. The features of each package may vary but most packages are able to:

FEATURE	FUNCTION
Import and place images	Bring images and photographs into your work, controlling the size and position.
Create shapes	Draw shapes (squares, oblongs ellipses and circles).
Change size	Increase or decrease the size of any part of your drawing.
Crop objects	Remove any part of an image that you do not require.
Select colour	Select a range of colours for any part of your design.
Rotate objects	Turn the position of any object by a number of degrees.
Flip objects	Flip a shape along its horizontal or vertical axis.
Copy objects	Copy an object as many times as you like.
Delete an object	Delete any part of the drawing, or you can delete the shapes. You will also be able to clear all the design.

FEATURE	FUNCTION
Fill shapes	Fill or flood a shape such as a square, a circle or an enclosed part of a design, with a pattern or colour.
Create effects	Apply shadow, alter transparency, fade out, distort or apply colour effects.
Touch up effects	Alter the brightness and contrast, correct the tint, blur or sharpen the images. You can also remove dust and scratches, clone areas and erase items.

GIVE IT A GO   working with images

1 Load your drawing program and the image file **DIAMOND** — your tutor will tell you where to find it.

2 Experiment with the features shown above.

3 Save the file using three of the formats that your program allows.

4 Compare the size of the files you have saved.

File formats

The file format is the way data is stored so that a program can open and save the file. The format is shown by a three-letter extension (such as .gif). The program may need to use a graphics filter.

- Enhanced Metafile (.emf)
- Graphics Interchange Format (.gif)
- Joint Photographic Experts Group (.jpg)
- Portable Network Graphics (.png)
- Microsoft Windows Bitmap (.bmp, .rle, .dib)
- Windows Metafile Graphics (.wmf)
- Tagged Image File Format (.TIF)
- Encapsulated PostScript (.eps)

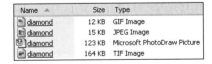

Figure 9.29 Image file formats

The format you choose dictates the size of your file. Figure 9.29 shows the image file DIAMOND. It has been saved in 4 formats. Notice the size of the file depending on the format chosen for saving it. This size of a file may be critical when you are carrying out your work, and if so you should note the relationship between format and size.

However, file size is not the only difference between graphic file formats. You can read more about file formats in Unit 10 Digital devices, page 175.

Audience

When you want to use an image, you must think about your audience and their needs. The more you know and understand about them, the better you can prepare. You should think about:

- who they are – their age, sex, educational background
- their knowledge and experience of the topic
- why they are there
- what they need to know.

This will affect the way in which you present material – if your audience is made up of 15- to 16-year-olds who have no experience of the topic, your approach will be different from that taken if it is for professionals who work in the topic field.

Your material must be of interest and relevant to your audience. This means it must be fit for purpose. This goes for images just as much as for the language. The language should be appropriate – for example, not too technical. For more advanced work, templates, house styles and formal layouts may also be related to suitability for purpose. Whatever you present should be new to your audience – a new subject or new information about a familiar subject.

To get and hold their attention, focus on what they need to know. Groups will have different concentration spans – make sure you take this into consideration.

◼◼◻ EVIDENCE ACTIVITY

A presentation using images

This activity will bring together your knowledge of a number of IT applications.

1   Gather together material to use for a presentation. Remember that the language and the graphics must be appropriate for the intended audience. You can select the topic from these options:

- A car manufacturer launching a new car to their car dealers.
- An introduction to your college for prospective students on an open day.
- A company informing its employees about changing suppliers.

2   Depending on the topic, you might want to prepare:

- background information for handouts and additional notes
- advertising flyers
- a product specification of the new car
- a spreadsheet identifying costs to be used as a slide
- spreadsheet data presented as a pie or bar chart
- images and photographs — of the car, the college or facilities such as the IT room.

3   Design a company logo and include it on the slides.

4   Produce a presentation of five or six slides.

5   Print a copy of the slides, audience notes, and any additional notes for the audience to take away.

6   What different software packages did you use in this case study?

7   Why did you use that software?

unit 10

Digital devices

This unit has been designed to give you the opportunity to use a range of digital devices — the devices used to record sound, and take images and the quality and speed of such devices. Use of images shortly after their capture is a great advantage — for example, sports photographers record key images during an event and send them immediately to the newspaper for publication in the next issue.

In this unit you will need to learn about:

- digital cameras
- scanners
- a range of additional digital devices currently available
- the impact of digital devices.

Digital cameras

We have been using cameras to record images since the late 1800s, when cameras were first used. These were plate cameras – each time a new picture (photograph) was required the film had to be changed. The next evolution was produced and introduced by Eastman Kodak – the Brownie. It was the first mass-produced, commercially available, cheap camera. The manufacturers then went on to develop products targeting different markets – including cameras for women. The next development was colour film, and in the 1980s disk cameras were introduced. Digital cameras are the latest development.

With digital cameras, instead of the light coming through the lens onto light-sensitive film, which is then wound on, the light falls onto digital light sensors which record and store the image as digital information.

The area of digital cameras is a rapidly changing area with many new developments. The market is not only dynamic, but also highly competitive. Like many developments the cost of digital cameras has decreased dramatically in the last few years. They are now within the reach of far more people.

• • • Advantages

A digital camera provides a moving image on the back of the unit on a LCD. You can take a picture and it is recorded onto the camera – if you do not like it you do not have to process it, you can delete it. If you want to retain the image you can then enhance it, alter it and process it in a number of different ways.

When digital cameras were introduced film cameras were still producing better quality results. However, the digital camera provides flexibility, instant results and it is cheaper as you do not have to buy more film.

Digital cameras have many advantages:

- You can view your pictures immediately – if you do not want a picture, you can delete it and take a new one. This is of particular use if you are taking photographs at a special event such as a wedding. You will want to be sure that you have the record of the event captured.
- You can take a lot more pictures because they are not all processed. For example, an architect may want to take several pictures of a site or buildings.
- You can share images via the Internet and emails. For example, you may want to send pictures to relatives or friends who can not share special events with you such as Christmas or a party.
- You can print images yourself on your computer, or take them in for normal processing.

Common digital terms

The language used in connection with digital devices can be a little confusing.
These are some of the commonly associated terms:

••• *Pixel*

The word Pixel is made up of the words **Pic**ture **el**ement. It means the smallest
element of a digitised image. One small dot among the many dots that make up an
image.

••• *Megapixel*

This means one million pixels. The more pixels in an image the greater the image
quality. A good average for an image is about two million pixels. The sensor size is
expressed in megapixels. The greater the number of megapixels, the more data the
sensor can capture and the more an image can be enlarged.

••• *Resolution*

This means the number of pixels in an image. The higher the number the higher the
quality of the image, and the higher the camera cost.

In addition to maximum resolution, look at the other resolution settings on a
camera. Many offer a range which can help to fit more pictures on a picture card or
save time making adjustments. For instance, if you intend using a particular picture
for email only, you could set the resolution setting low and not have to resize the
picture later.

If you think of a rectangle, the area is the length multiplied by the width. With a
digital camera sensor, the number of horizontal pixels times the number of vertical
pixels is the capture resolution.

Imagine that a camera has 2,160 horizontal pixels and 1,440 vertical pixels. When
the numbers are multiplied, the result is 3,110,400 pixels or 3.1 megapixels. This
table shows the ideal capture resolutions you need for the print sizes shown in
order to obtain a photo-quality picture.

Print Size		Required Capture Resolution
5×7 inches	15×20 cm	1 megapixel
8×10 inches	20×25 cm	2 megapixels
11×14 inches	28×36 cm	3 megapixels
20×30 inches	50×75 cm	4 megapixels

• • • *DPI*

This stands for Dots Per Inch. It means the number of dots a device can display per inch. For example:

- most laser printers have a resolution of 300 dpi
- most monitors have 72 dpi
- photo-quality inkjet printers range from 1200 to 2400 dpi.

• • • *PPI*

This stands for Pixels Per Inch. It means the number of pixels per inch indicates the image resolution. The higher this figure is, the more image detail and the higher the image quality. Note that:

- monitors display images at 72 ppi
- inkjet printers require at least 150 ppi for photo-realistic prints.

• • • *JPEG*

This stands for Joint Photographic Experts Group. It is a standardised format used by many digital cameras for storing images. This format is commonly used for images on the web and images attached to email messages. It is one of the most widely-used formats today.

• • • *LCD*

This stands for Liquid Crystal Display. It is a full-colour display screen on cameras used to preview and review pictures and view information, such as menu options and camera settings. You use the display screen to capture the image you require.

• • • *Memory card*

This is a storage device used to store data, such as picture and movie files. It is available in a range of sizes, such as 8 MB, 32 MB, and 256 MB.

• • • *Optical viewfinder*

This is how you view your subject with a digital camera. The optical viewfinder is similar in operation to viewfinders in traditional film cameras.

• • • *A photo kiosk*

This is a stand-alone computer-run system that allows users to edit and print pictures from negatives, prints, or digital files on a picture card, CD, or disk.

• • • *An on-line photo service*

This is a photo-finishing service that lets digital and, at some sites, film camera users share and store their photos in on-line photo albums and order high quality prints from digital images. The sites let users enhance pictures with editing tools, order prints on-line and order other photo products, like calendars and cards.

Cost of digital cameras

When you buy a digital camera the goal is to find a camera to take and use pictures easily, at a price you want to pay. The cost of digital cameras varies. Those at the low end of the range give low-resolution pictures suitable for email and monitor viewing but not for prints. Those at the high end give quality pictures and often have advanced functions. As the functions increase so do cost and complexity.

GIVE IT A GO   cost of digital cameras

The cost of digital cameras has come down dramatically in the last few years. They are now much less expensive, and range in price to suit all requirements. A person choosing a camera will need to consider the functions offered.

Find cameras in these price ranges and draw up a table showing the functions they offer, including, for example, the number of pixels. Suggest who may use the camera in each of the price ranges:

▷ £20–£30
▷ £60–£70
▷ £85–£95
▷ £150–£175
▷ £220–£250.

A range of digital cameras is now available at different prices

Uploading images to your computer

Before you can use or manipulate pictures, you need to get them onto a computer.

- Digital cameras are the quickest way to get digital pictures. To transfer pictures from a camera to a computer you can use either a docking station or a cable (see 'Connectivity', page 180).
- You can have your existing prints or negatives from a film camera digitised. These digital pictures will be placed on disk, or can be posted to an on-line album.
- You can use a scanner to scan your prints, and save the images in a suitable file format.
- You can scan prints with a picture maker. To do so you must take your print to a shop with a picture maker, scan and save it, then transfer it to the computer.
- You can get pictures onto a computer from a picture card. Connect the card reader to the computer, insert the picture card into it, and transfer the pictures.

Once you have the images on your computer, you can import them into a program to manipulate or present them.

Getting prints from digital pictures

• • • *Printing*

You can print your photographs yourself on an inkjet printer. You can choose glossy and satin surfaces. If you use glossy paper it will show greater detail. Satin finish will allow a softer finish. Your print will look just like a traditional photograph.

Use the correct paper in your printer. If you compare a picture printed on plain paper to the same picture printed on photo paper you will see what a difference there is. Plain paper absorbs and diffuses ink, dulling colour and blurring detail. The correct paper gives you better quality results in terms of colour and detail.

Usually you print images on a printer from your computer. However, some printers now allow you to insert your picture card into them to print images directly. Also, some digital cameras come with a 'station' that they dock in, which will print images directly.

• • • *Use an on-line photo service*

You can get traditional photo prints of your digital pictures from an on-line photo service. You transfer (upload) pictures from your computer to the on-line photo service. They will be displayed in an on-line album that shows the pictures at thumbnail size. You can use an on-line order form to identify those to print and the print size. Some services provide on-line editing software to make alterations or improvements to your pictures. Your prints will then be sent to you.

• • • *Use a picture maker*

You can make your own prints by using, for example, a Kodak picture maker – a kiosk about the size of a cash dispenser. You insert your picture card, a CD, or a diskette containing the images. If a digital file is not available you can scan your negative or print. Select the pictures you want to print and the print size. If required you can add borders, text messages, zoom, crop or enlarge your pictures, remove red eye, etc.

GIVE IT A GO   on-line photo services

1 Log on to the Internet.
2 Find out if there are any companies that offer on-line photo services in the UK.
3 Find out the closest picture-making facility to your location.

• • • *Connectivity*

If your computer is fairly new, a digital camera will probably work with it. However, before you buy a camera, check the specifications to find out what the computer requirements are. Most digital cameras require a USB (Universal Serial Bus) connection on the computer.

• • • *Firewire*

This is a thin cable that connects a camera to a computer or other device.

You may have seen the terms IEEE 1394 (named after the Institute of Electrical and Electronics Engineers), FireWire™ (a registered trademark of Apple), and i.Link™ (a trademark of Sony Electronics, Inc). They are all the same thing. When Apple first developed this system, it called it FireWire. When it was used in PCs and further developed, it was called the *IEEE 1394 High Performance Serial Bus.* Sony call it i.Link.

Whatever it is named this has become the standard digital audio/video interface for all digital video equipment. It allows you to transfer up to 400 Megabits per second, which makes it the fastest available connection between camcorders and other digital video hardware such as computers. This is because it transfers the information by optic fibre, not ordinary wire.

A Firewire connector is built into almost every digital camcorder. Because it adds cost to computers most manufacturers do not include them (although some have started to do so). With most PCs you need to add a Firewire card to the system. There are a number of companies that make such cards.

• • • *Other ports*

Parallel ports are not designed to be shared, that is, one device using the port and then another. Each device has a *driver*. Different drivers using the same parallel port causes problems. If a device such as a scanner is on a parallel port by itself it can work well. It is possible to add another separate port for another device, such as a printer.

Many printers have both USB and Parallel interfaces. Adding a USB cable to a printer allows for installation of the printer at a USB port, so avoiding any problem of printer and scanner not working on the same port.

• • • *Software*

Before you print your images or incorporate them into a document, you may want to adjust them. Basic picture-editing software gives you several easy methods of enhancing or improving your pictures. These are useful features to look for in a program:

- brightness and contrast adjustment
- colour adjustment
- rotating and flipping the image
- red-eye reduction
- cropping.

Different types of ports

GIVE IT A GO ## image-editing software

Using image-editing software, demonstrate your understanding of the terms above by using images. Present the *before* and *after* picture for each of the functions, with a brief explanation of its use.

When your experience with editing digital pictures goes beyond the routine such as fixing red eye, correcting colour, and adjusting the brightness and contrast, then you may want to consider more advanced techniques. Look for these features:

- different ways of selecting an object within your digital picture – rectangular and/or elliptical marquee, pen-type tool, lasso tool, colour selection wand
- sophisticated adjustments to your digital images and to each colour channel
- advanced cloning tools
- additional saving options
- transformation tools
- web-ready graphics creation.

More advanced features at a 'professional-level' give you even more options. This type of software is more expensive, and you may need to consider training to get the full benefits of it.

Image file formats

It is important that you choose the right file format to save your images. The commonly used formats are: GIF, JPG, PNG and TIFF.

Each format is suited to a specific type of image. For example, you need to use the correct format to get a small, fast-loading graphic for the web. When selecting the format you should be aware of the image quality and size.

● ● ● *GIF*

This format is used because of its size – it is small. It is used frequently on the Internet as it is ideal for small navigational icons and simple diagrams and illustrations where accuracy is required. This format saves with colour limitations, which makes it a poor format for photographic images.

The format can be animated – most animated banner advertisements are GIFs. You require an animation program to make your own animations. They can also be interlaced – a way of saving a graphic so that it loads progressively. A low detail version is loaded first and further layers of detail are added. This makes the file bigger but it means that a version of the image is placed on screen much more quickly.

• • • JPEG

This format (usually written without the 'E' as JPG), was designed for photographs. It is capable of displaying millions of colours.

You can save in this file format with zero per cent compression for a perfect image with a large file size, or with 60 per cent compression for a small but obviously degraded image. A compression setting of about 80 per cent will result in the best balance of quality and file size.

• • • PNG

This format (Portable Network Graphic) is specifically for the web. It was devised in response to a licensing scheme which meant the creators of any software that supported the GIF format had to pay $5,000 – a tax that has since expired.

This format is possibly better than the GIF format in many ways. Because this file type saves colour data more efficiently file sizes are smaller.

• • • TIFF

This format (Tagged Image File Format – also written TIF) was designed for the exchange of digital image data. The TIFF format originated in 1986 when Aldus Corporation and leading scanner vendors worked together to create a standard file format for images used in desktop publishing.

It is the most common format for popular imaging applications and in printing. It does not result in as small a file as a jpeg (which is why it is not used on the web), but image quality is higher.

• • • BMP

This is the standard Windows image format. It works well for pictures or graphics, but takes a lot of disk space because it is not a compressed format. It is the standard format for Windows wallpaper.

■■■ EVIDENCE ACTIVITY

Using images in a document

1 Choose a subject that you are interested in, and about which you have some text available.

2 Using a digital camera take some photographs (at least two) that would be appropriate to include.

3 Using software of your choice, produce a short article (1 page) about your chosen subject including the files you have created using the camera. You should change the size of one of the images, and rotate the other.

4 Provide copies of the original material to ensure that you have carried out the alterations.

5 Print your article.

 # Scanners

What can you do with a scanner?

- *Convert existing photographs* into digital images for use on web pages, for emailing, for bulletins and newsletters, for slides, and to print.
- *Copy documents.* Use a scanner and a printer as an alternative way of copying. You can also use the scanner controls to edit and improve the documents.
- *Fax documents.* You can fax text from a word processor, but if the text is printed in a book or magazine, you can scan it and then fax it. You can fax scanned images in the same way.
- *Scan documents and use OCR* (Optical Character Recognition) software to convert the image back to text. If you scan a page of text such as a magazine page, you will get a graphics image of the page. It is not text, it is a picture of the text, and can only be viewed or printed as an image. The purpose of OCR software is to decode the scanned image of the individual pixels to generate text characters. You can then load the file into a word processor.
- *Scan real items* – fabric or leaves can provide good textures to be used for web page backgrounds. The objects should be more or less flat.

Scanning software

Unlike a copier, a scanner does not create another piece of paper, but creates an image in memory. Once the image is in memory it can be displayed on the screen, saved or emailed. You must have the correct software to operate the scanner and which will also modify the images, i.e. alter the brightness, crop, resize, change colour, combine images, create special effects, etc.

To save a lot of time manipulating your images, most scanning software offers you different scanning settings – you can scan in colour, as greyscale (shades of black) or as Line art (black and white). You can also choose what resolution to scan at. Usually the software will scan a quick preview image so you can see if it will come out as you want it to, before you click for a full scan.

With the image as you want it, you can either print it or save it, or both. When saving, select a file format such as TIF or JPG. You then have an image that you can put on a website or email.

Types of scanner

• • • *Flatbed scanner*

A flatbed scanner is the most suitable choice for photo prints and documents. It is the most widely used. It is similar to a copier – it has a glass plate under a lid, and a moving light that scans across under it. It allows the scanning of photographs, paper documents, books, magazines, large maps, flat 3-D objects, and portions of documents larger than the scanner bed, such as maps. Most scan A4 size. A few can scan legal size documents, and a few have an A3 size bed.

• • • *Film scanner*

Film scanners give large images while retaining very good image quality. A film scanner allows you to scan film instead of the prints. Also called slide scanners, they can scan slides and negatives. Most are for 35 mm film. As the film is the original, the best results come from it.

If you want to print 35 mm slides or negatives in photo quality at 8×10 inch, A4 or larger, you will need a film scanner with 2700 dpi or more. They are more expensive, and more complex to use but give much better large images.

35 mm film scanners usually provide 2700 to 4000 dpi. 2700 dpi allows 8×10 inch prints. Image size and memory cost can be high when scanning film. This is because you are able to scan at very high resolution. To create enough pixels to print full page size, at least 128 megabytes of memory is required – more is better.

▩▩▩ EVIDENCE ACTIVITY

Using a scanner

1 Scan a photograph of yourself.

2 Save the image using three different file formats.

3 Print the image in the three different formats.

4 Comment on the differences in the size of the files and the quality of the output.

 # A range of additional digital devices

Digital video cameras

Digital video cameras are smaller and lighter than previous video tape cameras, and provide quality and ease-of-use. They are considered to be equal to or better than, professional analogue cameras costing far more. Digital video offers sharper image quality, and copies of digital videos (including copies of copies) are as sharp as the original.

Digital videos have CD quality audio. The colour system used retains three times as much colour which results in brighter, truer colours.

A digital camcorder's 'film' is called CCD. It captures the light falling on it and converts it to electrical signals. The surface is divided into pixels. CCDs are available in various sizes and resolutions. The higher the resolution, the sharper the images will be. Most cameras use a CCD with between 270,000 and 680,000 pixels.

A digital camera uses a lot of power when taking or playing back footage, especially when the LCD monitor is on. They require rechargeable batteries, and it is helpful to have spares, especially when travelling. You also need a charger and an AC adapter.

• • • *Choosing a camera*

When deciding on a camera it is important to investigate how it works, such as how the LCD screen swings and swivels, and how the controls work. Examine different cameras to see how accessible the buttons are, for example, how easy is it to begin recording, pause, or zoom?

• • • *Editing digital video*

Editing is simple – provided that your camera has a DV-in/out facility, the video can be transferred to the computer without conversion, edited, and then copied back to a digital tape. Not only is this simpler than analogue editing, there is no loss of image quality. You can also save the video data on the computer in a number of formats, and perhaps 'burn' it onto a CD or DVD. Once it is on the computer, you can send short clips as email attachments or post them on websites.

• • • *Editing functions*

Using software built into the camera, you can organise clips, trim them, and add effects and titles before playing them. These are some of the editing functions you should look for:

- *Scene Shuffle Mode*: This rearranges the order that video clips play back.
- *Scene Edit Mode*: This trims the length of a video clip to remove unwanted footage.

- *Scene Copy Mode*: This copies and inserts video clips.
- *Scene Transition Mode*: This provides a variety of effects and transitions to enhance your work. Transitions can appear from left to right, top to bottom, etc. and can fade in, wipe in, etc.
- *Drawing Layer Function*: This allows you to draw freehand on top of the video (like sports commentators).

• • • *Video features*

When selecting a camera, you may also want these features:

- *Time lapse*: This allows you to take frames at specified intervals to record things that happen over a long period of time – you may have seen this feature used to capture videos that speed up flowers blossoming.
- *Slow motion*: This mode takes more frames per second so that when the video is played back at the normal speed, it appears to go slowly. It is a very useful way for an athlete to analyse their action.
- *Remote control*: This allows you to operate recording and playback from a distance. You can use it to get yourself in the picture or to record wildlife that might be frightened off by your movement.
- *Infrared*: This allows you to film at up to about ten feet in total darkness. The scene is illuminated with an infrared beam from LEDs on the camera.

Camera phones

Camera phones are relatively new. They have a large number of features, which can include:

- *Photo caller ID*: This allows you to associate a picture with a person in your address book. It will then appear every time that person rings you
- *Wallpaper*: This allows you to save your favourite picture as the background
- *Self-timer*: This allows you to capture your picture at the right moment.

Camera phones are useful for spontaneous pictures, but they do not capture enough detail to make high quality prints. They allow you to:

- store and share your pictures regardless of time and location
- share your photos with any computer or photo-ready phone
- access all your saved pictures at any time
- send pictures directly to an account where you can use unlimited, secure storage for images and phone-captured video, on-line, and in one location
- use organisation and photo-editing tools.

As you will always be carrying your camera phone, you can capture spontaneous moments. As with a digital camera you can take a lot of pictures to increase your chance of capturing the right one. Delete any images not required. You can upload the images you do want to keep to your computer and store them.

Many allow you to choose the size of the pictures you take. They include a low, medium, and high setting for picture quality. Set it to the highest setting to capture the best quality pictures. You may not see a difference between the different quality settings on the display screen, but it will make a difference on a computer screen.

▣▣▣ EVIDENCE ACTIVITY

Digital devices: a presentation with images

1   Split your class into groups.

2   Each group should take one of the products below:
    - personal digital assistants (PDA) such as a palm pilot
    - MP3 players (such as the iPod)
    - minidisks
    - mobile phones
    - another digital device in which you have a particular interest.

3   Each member of the group should investigate a different aspect of the product. Combine your findings on the product.

4   Prepare a five-minute presentation, including images of the chosen item which you have scanned or photographed. You may want to improve or manipulate the images to suit the layout and design, and bearing in mind your audience. You may use any software applications you wish to present the information. (Information on these can be found in Unit 9.)

5   Present your findings to the group.

Latest developments

The use of digital devices has had a considerable impact, not only on society but also on individuals. In terms of society, one of the major developments has been the extensive use of digital cameras for monitoring town centres, railway stations and many business premises to deter crime. Another has been the development of computer communication, and the opportunity, therefore, for companies to allow employees to work from home, or to use employees in another part of the world.

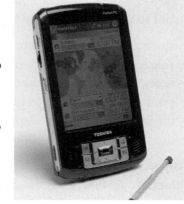

A pocket PC

In terms of the individual, the same developments in computer communication have allowed individuals to carry out many tasks from the home – e.g. banking and shopping. It has also allowed use of the Internet to a far wider group of individuals. This enables them to share views, opinions and help with other like-minded individuals or groups with similar interests.

GIVE IT A GO — the impact of digital devices

1 Split your class into groups.
2 Discuss the impact that you think digital devices have had on:
   • society
   • individuals.
3 Make a list of your points and present them to the other members of the class.

● ● ● *GPS – Global Positioning System*

One of the developments that has had an impact, not only on society, but also on individuals, is the use of digital device systems with satellites for monitoring purposes.

A Global Positioning System (GPS) is a satellite-based navigation system made up of a network of satellites. Used originally for military applications, the system is now available for many civilian applications. It can work in any weather conditions, anywhere in the world, 24 hours a day.

It is used in many industries including recreation (such as mountaineering and sailing), corporate vehicle fleet tracking, and surveying.

The system can determine, within 10–30 metres, the location of any device that has a GPS transceiver mounted. Having identified the location, an object's movements can be tracked, as it moves.

Vehicle tracking
One of the fast-growing uses is vehicle tracking. GPS-equipped fleet vehicles, public transportation systems, delivery vehicles, and courier services use receivers to monitor their locations at all times.

The Fire Service, Police, and emergency medical services, are using GPS receivers to determine the nearest service vehicle to an emergency, enabling the quickest response time using AVL. Automatic Vehicle Location is a method of remote vehicle tracking and monitoring using GPS.

Each vehicle has equipment that receives signals from a series of satellites. It calculates the current location, speed, and heading. This information can be stored for later retrieval or transmitted to a central control location where it is displayed on a high-resolution map.

Car-makers are installing moving-map displays guided by GPS receivers. Any vehicle that is equipped can be provided with a range of support services to make every journey as quick, easy and safe as possible. Using the system you can supply details of your destination to a central computer, and in a very short time the route is sent to your car. You will also receive traffic data and the latest mapping information. The information can be displayed on a screen in your car or through synthesised voice instructions.

vehicle tracking

GPS systems are used widely within the security field to protect people and property – for example:

A lorry fitted with a vehicle-tracking device was stolen in Somerset. The vehicle was fully loaded. The tracking company were contacted and were able to locate the vehicle and download the historical data. This information revealed that the vehicle had travelled to London. It had stopped for some time before travelling on to a location close to J10 of the M6 where it was abandoned. The police were provided with all the details. Using the information they were able to identify the exact location the cargo had been unloaded. The cargo and vehicle were recovered.

 # The impact of digital devices

The latest developments in digital devices point to an increasing impact that they are having on society and individuals. We will now explore the impact they are also having on the workplace.

investigate the workplace

In order that you can see the impact first hand, it would be very useful if you could organise a visit to a local magazine company or your local newspaper. This would help you to understand how the magazine or paper is put together, the technology and software available, and how it is used.

The leisure industry

• • • *News gathering*

News gathering has changed dramatically. Consider the reporting of wars and how much it has changed because of the technology now available. As an example, consider the reporting of the Second World War and the recent war in Iraq. During the Second World War reporters were not 'on the spot'. Communications could take weeks or months to be reported. Servicemen had to rely on letters to communicate with their families and friends – and these could also take weeks or months to arrive.

Now consider the reporting of the war in Iraq. Reporters were present in the field. We could watch the war unfolding on our television sets, and join in debates on the Internet. The reporters, in some instances, were using hand-held picture phones to send their reports. Servicemen were not only seen in the action as it happened, but they also had the facility of using mobile phones to keep in touch with their family and friends.

● ● ● *The photographic and film industries*

The photographic and film industries have been affected by digital cameras and the way that we can produce prints, either at home on the Internet or in other facilities around the country. One of the criticisms, however, about the use of digital images is the manner in which they can be manipulated. Images can be modified in such a way as to be misleading, or touched up to provide perfect images of models that remove any 'flaws'. One of the major manufacturers of cameras have announced that they will only be selling *digital* cameras in the UK, although they will continue to produce film for SLR cameras.

● ● ● *The music industry*

The music industry has been greatly affected by the widespread sharing of music on the Internet.

Not only has the way we acquire music changed, but also how we use it, store it and listen to it. The latest digital music players, so light they can easily be carried in a pocket, can hold up to 10,000 songs, thousands of digital photos and work as personal voice recorders. They are fully compatible with PCs.

The manufacturing industry

Manufacturing and design has been impacted by the introduction of CAD and CAM – Computer Aided Design and Computer Aided Manufacture. Many production processes are now carried out by computers. This has led to an increase in production speed, which means that more goods can be produced, by less people, in a shorter time. In most cases this has led to a drop in the number of people required to run the systems. The automation of processes can be seen in many industries including car, and other machine production.

Servicing has also been impacted. At one time you would take your car to a garage and a mechanic would investigate any faults. Today, many manufacturers have diagnostic computers to determine engine and performance problems. These advances, while having a negative impact on employment have increased the productivity of the remaining workforce. They are freed from routine work to carry out more refined processes requiring human intervention.

The professional services industry

There are very few places where digital devices are not in use, from scanners at the check-out that can automatically update stock levels and re-order automatically, to automated processes in manufacture. The impact of the technology on professional services has also helped to provide quicker access to data, to reduction in costs and to increases in productivity. The use of the technology ideally results in fewer personnel being required to carry out routine time-consuming tasks. For example:

• • • *Estate agents*

Once the details of a property are entered onto a database the information can be shared with all branches of the company, and also placed on the website. This allows quicker and easier access to the information and for prospective buyers to view that information without having to visit a branch, and at a time convenient to them – such as in the evening when the branches are closed.

• • • *The medical profession*

As patient records are now computerised, this allows medical records to be shared by different groups. At one time, the records held at your doctor's surgery could only be seen there. Today, depending on the communication links with Health authorities, they can also be seen by doctors if you are admitted to hospital. This way they have the full medical history available to them. In some places, prescriptions can be placed directly with pharmacists, and you simply have to go and pick up that prescription.

• • • *The travel industry*

Many people now make their own arrangements for their holiday and travel arrangements – usually on the Internet. With low-cost airlines, and the ability of companies and hotels to advertise directly on the Internet, costs have been reduced. This has had an impact on travel agents.

• • • *The legal profession*

Digital devices have been introduced into the legal profession to allow quicker communication of documents between members of the legal profession. Court proceedings are still recorded by hand, but there are moves to change this. One advance has been the use of video links that allow vulnerable witnesses to give evidence without having to be in the court itself. This is used particularly for young children who may be frightened in a court.

▨▨▨ EVIDENCE ACTIVITIES

Digital devices in the workplace

1   Split your class into groups.

2   Each group should provide two further examples of how digital devices could be used in:
- the medical field
- the travel industry
- the legal profession.

3   Each group should also consider how the introduction of those digital devices could cut costs in each fields, increase productivity or provide a better service. Each group should present points to the other members of the class.

4   Each group should present points to the other members of the class.

5   Using a suitable application, combine the feedback from all the groups.

6   Once the file is printed, add it to your evidence file.

Index